# The Peasants' Revolting...Crimes

This book is dedicated to Mr and Mrs Peasant,
the forgotten and abused (but unvanquished)
heroes of history

# The Peasants' Revolting...Crimes

## A disrespectful history of the criminal acts committed by the underclasses of Britain

Terry Deary

PEN & SWORD
HISTORY

First published in Great Britain in 2019 by
Pen & Sword History
An imprint of
Pen & Sword Books Ltd
Yorkshire – Philadelphia

ISBN 978 1 52674 557 6

A CIP catalogue record for this book is
available from the British Library.

Printed and bound by CPI Group (UK) Ltd, Croydon, CR0 4YY


Pen & Sword Books Limited incorporates the imprints of Atlas, Archaeology,
Aviation, Discovery, Family History, Fiction, History, Maritime, Military, Military
Classics, Politics, Select, Transport, True Crime, Air World, Frontline Publishing, Leo
Cooper, Remember When, Seaforth Publishing, The Praetorian Press, Wharncliffe
Local History, Wharncliffe Transport, Wharncliffe True Crime and White Owl.

For a complete list of Pen & Sword titles please contact

PEN & SWORD BOOKS LIMITED
47 Church Street, Barnsley, South Yorkshire, S70 2AS, England
E-mail: enquiries@pen-and-sword.co.uk
Website: www.pen-and-sword.co.uk

Or

PEN AND SWORD BOOKS
1950 Lawrence Rd, Havertown, PA 19083, USA
E-mail: Uspen-and-sword@casematepublishers.com
Website: www.penandswordbooks.com

# Contents

*Law grinds the poor, and rich men rule the law.*
Oliver Goldsmith (1728–1774),
Irish novelist, playwright and poet

*It is the duty of righteous men to make war on all undeserved privilege, but one must not forget that this is a war without end.*
Primo Levi (1919–1987) – Italian writer,
and Holocaust survivor

*The criminal is with us throughout the ages. He is with us still, though in much reduced numbers, for the farther we go in history the more criminals we find.*
Bishop Fraser, Professor of Mediaeval and Ecclesiastical
History, University of Manchester lecture, 1919

# Introduction

*When beggars die, there are no comets seen;*
*The heavens themselves blaze forth the death of princes.*
                    William Shakespeare (1564 – 1616), *Julius Caesar*

Will Shakespeare. Great writer, dodgy historian. And, let's be honest, a bit of a snob. A lot of princely corpses litter his stages by the end of his plays – and a few princessly ones too.

But no comets for dead commoners. Great crimes for the lords and ladies but minor crimes are left to the lower classes. The peasants.

> *PEASANT: A poor smallholder or agricultural labourer of low social status.*
> *(Informal) An ignorant, rude, or unsophisticated person.*
>                                             Dictionary

Autolycus, in *A Winter's Tale*, is a con artist who wanders around the Bohemian countryside taking advantage of any mug he happens to come across. He is also a comical character. Autolycus is one of the 'masterless men' of Tudor England – the impoverished and homeless who wandered the countryside. Many pretended to be disabled or mentally ill, so they could beg for food and cash.

A peasant-criminal. WHY did they do it? Shakespeare the sociologist may have been saying it was due to the increasing enclosure of land in the countryside. As land was closed off for grazing livestock, there was less land for communal farming purposes. That left peasants, like Autolycus, no means of supporting themselves and/or their families.

### Vile violence

Shakespeare was an entertainer. His audiences demanded dramatic crimes and he wrote them by the bucketful ... crimes mostly committed by the upper classes. Maybe audiences were looking for a better class of crime?

*Titus Andronicus* begins with state-sanctioned execution, and becomes increasingly violent with rape and mutilation, and climaxes in cannibalism – heads and hands are cut off, on stage. Sons ...

> *... baked in a pie*
> *Whereof their mother has daintily fed.*[1]

A young Roman noblewoman, Lavinia, has her tongue cut out to stop her blabbing about her rape, and allows the Elizabethan audiences to enjoy the revolting poetry like Lavinia's uncle, Marcus:

> *Alas, a crimson river of warm blood,*
> *Like to a bubbling fountain stirred with wind,*
> *Doth rise and fall between they rosed lips,*
> *Coming and going with thy honey breath.*

---

1. Some critics interpret eating your sons, not so much as 'cannibalism' as 'incest'. Whatever the legality of eating your children, just don't try it at home.

She has her hands cut off too, and that provides a bit of a laugh for her rapists and mutilators who mock her.

CHIRON:       *Go home, call for sweet water, wash thy hands.*
DEMETRIUS: *She hath no tongue to call, nor hands to wash,*
               *And so let's leave her to her silent walks.*
CHIRON:       *And 'twere my cause, I should hang myself.*
DEMETRIUS: *If thou hadst hands to help thee knit the cord*

And like any good morality tale, the criminals make a big mistake. They forget that Lavinia can write. Lavinia holds a stick in her mouth and spells out the names of the rapists, Demetrius and Chiron.[2]

At a dinner banquet, Lavinia is killed by her loving dad, Titus. His motive is not one you'd find in many whodunits. He says he wants her 'shame' to die along with his 'sorrow' for her.

In other words, he's doing the lass a favour … while assuaging his own sorrow? That's all right then.

*Peasant pleasure*

The majority of Shakespeare's audience would be the groundlings – the lower classes who stood there for a couple of hours to be entertained by tales of crime and cruelty. He explored motivation among his murderers:

---

2. And talking of morality, Lavinia is no angel. She watches as her father cuts Chiron and Demetrius's throats. With her stumps, she holds a bowl to catch the blood, so her father can use it to make a human meat pie for the murderers' mother's dinner.

| Hamlet | – Revenge |
|---|---|
| Lady Macbeth | – Ambition |
| Othello | – Jealousy |
| Brutus | – Power |

… and so on. These flawed heroes were all upper-class lords and ladies, and their crimes were enjoyed by the underclasses. Since Ancient Greek days, when Oedipus killed his dad and married his mum, our fictional crime has been dominated by the noble nutters and high-class criminals.

Charles Dickens redressed the balance with a look at low-life London crime that shows us the poor have as much criminal excitement as the rich:

> 'Stop thief. Stop thief.' There is a human passion for hunting something deeply implanted in the human breast. One wretched, breathless child, panting with exhaustion, terror in his looks, agony in his eye, large drops of perspiration streaming down his face, strains every nerve to make head upon his pursuers; and as they follow on his track, and gain upon him every instant, they hail his decreasing strength with still louder shouts, and whoop and scream with joy 'Stop thief'. – Ay, stop him for God's sake, were it only in mercy.
>
> Charles Dickens (1818–1870),
> British writer and social critic, *Oliver Twist*

Read Agatha Christie (or any of her 'Golden Age' contemporaries) you'd be convinced that the elite eliminators would wipe out the genteel within a generation. When the posh weren't killing their refined friends then they were coming to sticky ends themselves – often on the gallows. Yes, there *are* a few working-class victims, but they are often there for comic effect. A servant died in an undignified way …

*Strangled, she was, with a stocking round her throat – been dead for hours, I'd say. And, sir, it's a wicked kind of joke – there was a clothes peg clipped on her nose …*
        Agatha Christie (1890 – 1976), English writer, *A Pocket Full of Rye* (Miss Marple)

An aristocrat wouldn't suffer that sort of undignified end in a Christie story, would s/he? If Christie's tales were true there'd be more bodies than books in the country house libraries and the middle classes would have exterminated themselves by now.

If crime fiction is dominated by the upper classes, then crime fact has been peopled by the lower classes. To discover *who* and *what* and *why*, we need to dig into the more obscure pages of historical record.

*Treat all men alike. Give them the same law. Give them an even chance to live and grow.*
        Chief Joseph (1840 – 1904), Native American leader

It would be interesting to sample a history of crime among the underclasses. Surely, they must be as interesting as Christie's fictional fiends? And, like Shakespeare, they must tend towards the entertainingly revolting.[3]

A sort of *Peasants' Revolting Crimes*. But where would you find such a book?

---

3. The *Daily Mail* reported on 1 May 2014 that at a performance at the Globe Theatre of *Titus Andronicus*: 'As Lavinia – whose tongue and hands are cut off after she is raped – appeared on stage at Shakespeare's Globe, five people fainted, while others complained of feeling sick and fearing sleepless nights.' So, readers of this book are warned, there may be some scenes that they may find distressing, blah, blah …

# Chapter 1

# Norman Nastiness

*It is the custom in England, as with other countries, for the nobility to have great power over the common people, who are serfs. This means that they are bound by law and custom to plough the field of their masters, harvest the corn, gather it into barns, and thresh and winnow the grain; they must also mow and carry home the hay, cut and collect the wood, and perform all manner of tasks of this kind.*

Jean Froissart (1337 – c.1405), French-speaking mediaeval author and court historian (written in 1395)

From the earliest societies there seems to have been a layering of human power. Egyptian pharaohs lived royally and went on to a wonderful afterlife while the underclasses laboured and died to build the extravagant tombs.

But it was the Normans who gave the layering a shape – the feudal system. Kings at the top down to serfs and peasants at the bottom. After a little dust-up called the Battle of Hastings they had carte blanche to create their rigid society in England. The king owned everything and the descending orders 'paid' with 'service' and/or cash.

*William next invented a system according to which everybody had to belong to someone else, and everybody else to the king. This was called the Feutile System.*

Sellars and Yeatman, *1066 And All That*

It was easy to spot the peasants because they were the conquered Saxons, living in wattle-and-daub huts with no windows, while the lords (and top clergy) sat in their castles and the monarchs in their palaces. The lords were invariably Norman.

Not only did Mr and Mrs Peasant pay rent and service for his land to the lord, they had to pay a tax to the church, a tithe. This was a 10 per cent tax on all of the farm produce they had produced in that year.

## Immoral earnings

*Someone once said that politics is the second-oldest profession. I'm beginning to think it bears resemblance to the first.*

Ronald Reagan (1911 – 2004),
actor and 40th President of the US

Follow the logic of this: Adam and Eve ate the apple in the Garden of Eden and discovered they were naked. They fashioned clothes for themselves. So, what is the world's oldest profession? Tailor?

*Of all the professions that ever were nam'd,*
*The taylor's, though slighted, is much to be fam'd:*
*For various invention, and antiquity,*
*No trade with the tayler's comparèd may be.*

The Song in Praise of the Merchant-Taylors,
London, 1680

Around the 1900s, Rudyard Kipling wrote a story about a prostitute and quoted the Bible to 'prove' that prostitution was the world's oldest profession.

*Joshua son of Nun sent two spies with orders to reconnoitre the country. The two men came to Jericho and went to the house of a prostitute named Rahab.*

The Book of Joshua 2:1

Kipling's claim that prostitution was the oldest profession became the received wisdom of the world. Prudes and prigs have always enjoyed being shocked by prostitution and seen it as a crime. Yet men of power and/or wealth have chosen to ignore the morality of exploiting a cash-poor woman. The men of power have generally escaped the opprobrium of society ... not to mention the legal punishments.

So, it is a perverse pleasure to hear a tale of a peasant prostitute who turned the tables on the powerful.

## The priest and the peasant

Christmas is a 'quarter day' – no, that doesn't mean it's six hours long. It is one of the four days in the year day when rents were paid to the landowners and landlords.

In Well, near Richmond in North Yorkshire, in 1289 the parish priest had a very comfortable arrangement with a local peasant woman. She would see to his carnal needs and receive a pittance. The church system of tithes meant the priest was a wealthy man who chose to ignore his own teachings.

*And again I say unto you, It is easier for a camel to go through the eye of a needle, than for a rich man to enter into the kingdom of God.*

Matthew 19:24, King James Bible[1]

---

1. Yes, you are right, the King James Bible hadn't been dreamt of in 1289 and this priest's Bible would have been in Latin. But it's the thought that counts. He was filthy rich as well as filthy ... and Jesus would not have approved.

The cloud to his silver lining was that he'd lose his treasures if the authorities found out about his live-in lover.

He was expecting a visit from the king's rent collector on Christmas Day that year – the last quarter day. The rent collector would expect to stay the night. The rent collector would report the parson to the king if he saw the woman living at the rectory. She had broken her ties with her disapproving family in the village, so she had nowhere else to go.

There was only one place secure enough to keep her hidden for the duration of the visit: the parson stuck the young woman in his strong room.

The girl had food, drink and a candle. She had forgotten to take a chamber pot into the room with her ... something that would work to her advantage.

For, when she looked around the room, she found it was stuffed with the tithe money. Soon it was her dress that was stuffed with money. She slipped a fat purse down the front of her dress. Then it was just a matter of escaping from the locked room. The lack of a chamber pot gave her an idea. 'Let me out,' she cried. 'I need a pee.'

The panicking parson needed her to keep quiet, so he unlocked the door. What did the girl do? Ran off with the money. Of course, the king's rent collector was furious that his money was missing.

The parson got the blame ... and the sack.

The peasant concubine? We don't know. But the immoral among us have to hope she escaped with the hard-earned cash and lived happy ever after.

*About morals, I know only that what is moral is what you feel good after and what is immoral is what you feel bad after.*
Ernest Hemingway (1899–1961), American novelist

## Arson

*All religion, my friend, is simply evolved out of fraud, fear, greed, imagination, and poetry.*
Edgar Allan Poe (1809 – 1849), American writer

The parsons didn't just pay rents to the Crown on quarter days. They also *collected* them from the peasantry, of course. In the parish of Sedgefield – separated from the Richmond parson by 25 miles and 500 years – that collecting caused a problem for the rector's wife.

In the fortnight before Christmas the rector did a rash and foolish thing and died. His wife knew that the money due to her thoughtless hubby would be withheld by the tenants of the church lands. It would go to her husband's successor.

She had failed to keep the old Church of England chump alive. Maybe she could keep up the *illusion* of his being alive … just long enough for the rents to be paid? The tenants would queue at the table in the hall of the vicarage and put their money down on the table in front of the vicar.

It would be easy enough to darken the room … 'The vicar has a terrible headache and can't stand strong light,' would do as an excuse.

But the smell of his decomposing body may give the game away. The ingenious woman solved that – she immersed the corpse in vinegar for the days leading up to Christmas. He was well and truly pickled.

On the quarter day she rinsed off the corpse, dressed it and propped it in his chair, then opened the door to the tenants. They were a little perturbed by the lingering scent of vinegar but paid up.

Next day, Boxing Day, the news was all around the village of Sedgefield. 'The Rector is dead,' they said. 'A day too late,' they groaned.

But the doctor gave the game away to the farmers drowning their disappointment in the tavern. 'I examined the body. Dead at least two weeks, I'd say.'

The furious farmers smelled a rat ... or rather, a pickled rector. They took their ale-filled bodies up the road to the rectory. The doctor tried to tell them that the rector's wife had left on the six o'clock stagecoach to York, but they didn't listen. The sky glowed golden ahead of them. The villagers stopped and stared up at the burning building.

Most of the rectory was swallowed by the fierce flames. Only one tower window was still dark. As the folk looked up a greenly glowing face looked down on them. 'The parson. The pickled parson's pickled ghost,' a woman screamed before flames burst through the tower and it collapsed into the shattered shell of the house.

The rectory is gone, but the tale of the pickled parson lives on in Sedgefield.

Was the vicar's wife an arsonist as well as a fraud? If so, she is lucky she didn't live in 2018. *The Times* newspaper came up with an alarming headline:

*Punishment for arson to match crime*
*The Times*, 27 March 2018

Really? So that means if you are convicted of arson the police will set you alight?[2]

## Animal theft

*Sheep rustling is often seen as an amusing or old-fashioned crime. But as thieves who stole £35,000 worth of livestock*

---

2. Rather more prosaically, *The Times'* article suggested tougher penalties were to be introduced for arson, not that the criminal would be burned at the stake.

*from farms on both sides of the Pennines are jailed, what is the true cost of fleecing the farming community?*

*Since cavemen first kept goats, rustlers have targeted livestock owners.*

*And though it is one of the oldest felonies on record, it shows no signs of abating.*

BBC News, 7 January 2016

'Since cavemen first kept goats'? Cavemen are classified as pre-historic, so how does the reporter know this? It must be an awesome piece of research by that BBC reporter.

Someone once defined historians as being 'as seedy and devious as politicians', but maybe BBC reporters can be added to that hall of shame?

Nowadays the peasant rustlers in northern England have the M6 as a fast route out of the county. They operate in organised gangs, and have lorries, quad bikes and well-trained sheepdogs. The real victims of the crime could end up on your dinner table.

The punishment for the convicted English rustlers? Jail for a year or two. But those convicted rustlers are so very lucky.

In the 1200s, Peter of Clarendon 'did steal a horse to the value of 2 shillings'. That 10p horse cost him his life.

The case was brought before the Sheriff of Wiltshire. A 'sheriff' is an old English word shortened from 'shire-reeve' – the law-enforcement officer for a county (or shire) on behalf of the king. These sheriffs had enormous power.

*Unlimited power corrupts the possessor.*
William Pitt the Younger (1759–1806),
British Prime Minister

Marino Branch
Brainse Marino
Tel: 833629

7

Robin Hood may be a fictional character – as you know, Robbing Hood was the vigilante champion of the peasants.[3] But most sheriffs, like Robin's wicked Sheriff of Nottingham, were far from fictional. The majority of them just couldn't help exploiting their position to persecute the poor. If Robin Hood didn't exist, then he should have done.

'Dunking' a suspect in a pond or river is usually thought of as a test for the guilt of a witch. It had wider uses in Norman times. The Sheriff of Wiltshire had a pit dug and filled with water, which was then blessed by a priest. Peter of Clarendon was thrown in. If he sank he was innocent – probably drowned, but innocent.

The unfortunate Peter floated and was therefore guilty. He was taken out and executed. But the Sheriff was almost certainly as bent as all his fellow sheriffs.

*A sheriff walks into a saloon, and shouts for everyone's attention. 'Has anyone seen Brown Paper Jake?' he asks. 'He wears a brown paper hat, a brown paper waistcoat, a brown paper shirt, brown paper boots, brown paper pants, and a brown paper jacket.'*

*'So, what's he wanted for?' asks the barman.*

*'Rustlin'' replies the sheriff.*

### Henry II's lawmaker

Another sheriff, Sheriff Ranulf Glanville, was the law enforcer for Yorkshire, Warwickshire and Leicestershire from 1163 to 1170. He was a great advocate of dunking and killed 120 men in this way. The executed criminals' possessions were taken by the court, and that gives a clue as to his enthusiasm for dunking.

---

3. He and his gang robbed the rich because the poor had nothing worth pinching.

Ranulf was initially promoted by the king for his good work. He became legal adviser to Henry II and even ran the country while Henry went over the Channel to bash the French. This man who wrote the laws used the loopholes for his own profit.

Then, along with the majority of his peasant-robbing high sheriffs, he was sacked for corruption. He abused his position to peculate ...

*PECULATION: The act of illegally taking or using money, especially public money, that you are responsible for managing.*

Dictionary

Cue cheering peasants. But despite this conviction, rather remarkably, he went on advising Henry on the law. And what harsh laws they were.

If you're a peasant like Peter who steals a 10p horse, you die. If you are a lord like Ranulf who steals thousands, then you sail serenely over the choppy stretch of water. He was reinstated as Sheriff of Yorkshire, of course.

Ranulf joined one of Richard I's Crusades and died at the Siege of Acre in 1190. This was no consolation to rustler Peter of Clarendon or the other 120 victims of his abuse.

It's not surprising the peasants fulminated against the Norman oppressors and dreamed of a Robin Hood. The surprise is it took them another 200 years before they actually rebelled.

## Football violence

*I'd be surprised if all 22 players are on the field at the end of the game – one's already been sent off.*

George Best (1946 – 2005),
Northern Irish professional footballer

9

During the 1970s, football thugs began to organise themselves into 'firms' with charming names like Suicide Squad, Chelsea Headhunters, Everton County Road Cutters and Hull City Psychos, as well as the quaint Stoke City Naughty Forty and the almost cute Queen's Park Rangers Bushbabies.

Yet these 'firms' were not the sons of peasant stock. The 1970s 'firms' had become gentrified. ('Arsenal have by far the most middle-class supporters,' an Arsenal fan proudly claims.) The middle classes filched football hooliganism from the poor.

Criminal violence and football has a long and dishonourable history. Like most things, it started with the Normans. Look at the history …

### Hoofing hooligans

⇨ 1100s  Mob football stormed into England around the twelfth century. Villages would challenge one another to a Shrove Tuesday match. Both teams rush for the ball and try to score by kicking the ball over the other team's goal line. No murder or manslaughter allowed. Apart from that … no rules really. It caught on to such an extent it was banned by Royal decree by many kings and queens.

> *Two towns, that long that war had raged*
> *Being at football now engaged*
> *For honour, as both sides pretend,*
> *Left the brave trial to be ended*
> Charles Cotton (1630–1687), English poet

⇨ 1174  A Shrove Tuesday mob-football match in London was explained as:

*All the youth of the city go to a flat patch of ground ... for the famous game of ball. ... the workers of each guild are also seen carrying their own ball. The older citizens, fathers, wealthy citizens, come on horseback to watch the younger men competing.*

William Fitzstephen (d.1191), English cleric

⇨ 1280   The game known as 'Camp Ball' was similar to football. You grabbed the ball and tried to get it into your opponents' goal a few dozen metres or a couple of miles apart. There were any number on each side and hardly any rules. The trouble was there were no football strips – players wore their normal clothes ... including knives. In Newcastle upon Tyne in 1280, Henry de Ellington ran into David le Keu. David was wearing a knife at his belt; the knife stabbed Henry in the gut and he died. Deadly David didn't get a red card but hacked Henry probably got a very red shirt. That incident was accidental, but mob-football could often be used as a form of wild justice – scores could be settled under cover of 'play'. Some village/town disputes were dealt with by two large groups of men supposedly trying to get the ball and kick it against a church door. It was recorded that players would perish in the ensuing battle. The presence of a ball was almost secondary to this opportunity for settling old feuds and land disputes. Old scores, not football scores, were what mattered.

⇨ 1314   Edward II became involved in the debate on football and in 1314 complained about:

> *certain tumults arising from great footballs in the fields of the public, from which many evils may arise.*

⇨ 1388    Henry IV was the next monarch who tried to stop England's young men from playing football when he issued a new ban in 1388. This was ineffective and in 1410 his government imposed a fine of 20 shillings and six days' imprisonment on those caught playing football. (Some fans believe this law should be brought back for certain players in their team today.)

⇨ 1457    Miserable James II of Scotland banned football and golf, saying:

> *If the men want to practise a sport then they should try something useful, like archery.*

In 1460, James II was having a siege at Roxburgh Castle. He ordered the firing of his cannon to welcome his wife to the siege. One cannon exploded, blew his leg off, and that was the full-time whistle for Jim. A lesson to us all about what happens when you take your eye off the ball.

⇨ 1471    A few centuries later, another monk wrote that football was:

> *The game at which they had met for common recreation is called by some the foot-ball-game. It is one in which young men propel a huge ball not by throwing it into the air, but by striking and rolling it along the ground, and that not with their hands but with their feet.*
>
> *A game, I say, abominable enough and, in my judgement, more common, undignified and worthless than any other kind of game, rarely ending but with some loss, accident or disadvantage to the players themselves.*
>
> Monk at Caunton, Nottinghamshire

⇨ 1531   The Puritan preacher Thomas Elyot argued that football:

> *causes beastly fury and extreme violence.*

Another Tudor writer said:

> *Every player lies in wait to knock down the other players or punch them on the nose. Sometimes the players' necks are broken, sometimes their backs, sometimes their arms and legs. Sometimes their noses gush with blood. There are no rules that I can tell. The man with the ball must run with it for his life.*

Sometimes football was banned because fights broke out among the spectators watching the game. A precursor to today's football hooliganism?

King Henry VIII, however, is believed to have been a keen player. You can understand why an odious psychopath would be drawn to that sort of sport, can't you? In the divorce game he changed the rules to make sure he won – when the Pope refused to penalise Katherine of Aragon (and let Anne Boleyn on as a sub) the obese ogre simply made himself the ref. In the metaphor of football, he moved the goalposts.

⇨ 1583   Puritan Stubbes said:

> *Football may rather be called a friendly kinde of fight, than a play, or recreation; a bloody and murthering practice, than a fellowly sporte or pastime.*[4]

---

4. Obviously written on a day when his spell-checker was malfunctioning.

⇨ 1589    The records show that young men refused to accept the banning of football. In 1589, Hugh Case and William Shurlock were fined 2 shillings for playing football in St Werburgh's cemetery during the vicar's sermon. A really grave offence.

⇨ 1606    One of the deadliest Shakespeare insults of all came in his *King Lear*:

*Thou base football-player*

⇨ 1608    In Manchester in 1608, a few years before Alex Ferguson took over the team:

*a company of lewd and disordered persons ... broke many men's windows during unlawful game of football.*

⇨ 1618    It was such a major problem that in 1618 the local council appointed special 'football officers' to police these laws. Certainly the king at the time, James I, thought the game ill-suited to an aristocrat. It was a game for 'country swaines'. Football violence was definitely attributed to the peasantry back then.

⇨ 1700s   According to one student at Westminster, a public school, the violence wasn't the exclusive purview of the peasantry. Those public school chaps could mix it with the best of them. The football played at his school was very rough and involved a great deal of physical violence:

*When running ... the enemy tripped, shinned, charged with the shoulder, got down and sat upon you ... in fact did anything short of murder to get the ball from you.*

⇨ 1801   As the Industrial Revolution pulled peasants into
          towns of the dark satanic mills – and away from their
          country pleasures and open fields, the game was
          heading for extinction.

> *Football was formerly much in vogue among
> the common people of England, though of late
> years it seems to have fallen into disrepute.
> When the exercise becomes exceeding violent,
> the players kick each other's shins without
> the least ceremony, and some of them are
> overthrown at the hazard of their limbs.*
>
> Joseph Strutt, engraver and antiquary, 1801

⇨ 1811   Football games were often organised in the street.
          Two sides booted a leather ball filled with air and
          weren't too bothered about how many windows they
          broke in houses and coaches. In Gloucester in 1811,
          the *Shrewsbury Chronicle* reported ...

> *An apprentice was convicted of playing
> football on a Sunday. He was sentenced to
> fourteen days in prison.*

The crime was clearly breaking the Sabbath, not
booting a ball.

⇨ 1830   Football was kept alive by Irish workers in Islington,
          where ...

> *Some fine specimens of wrestling are sometimes
> exhibited.*
>
> *Everyday Book*, 1830

⇨ 1846    Violent outbreaks were reported at matches, with the riot act having to be read out at a game in Derby in 1846.

⇨ 1881    The peasant game was encouraged by the ruling class and had benefits. In 1881, Sir Watkin Williams-Wynn, MP for Denbighshire, argued:

> *Much has been said of the British spending their time on drinking. These kinds of sports keep young men from wasting their time. After playing a good game of football young men are more glad to go to bed than visiting the public house.*

So football is credited with SAVING the workers from the evils of liquor. Who'd have thought it?

## Knife crime

*KNIFE CRIME: noun: knife crime; plural noun: knife crimes criminal offences committed using a knife as a weapon.*

Dictionary

In 2018, a spate of knife crimes in London puzzled the police and panicked the public. Young men were killing one another on an alarming scale. London's murder rate had risen 40 per cent in only three years, and by February was higher than the homicide rate in New York for the first time in history.

*Fatal stabbings are taking place every three days in London amid fears of the resurgence of 'postcode wars' between rival gangs.*

*The Independent,* 30 March 2018

A former police leader said there should be more police on the streets. Wise words, but there was one idea that was never even suggested:

⇨ Bring all the rival gangs together.
⇨ Arm each man equally with a single knife.
⇨ Place them in a confined space.
⇨ Let them fight until one gang is eliminated.
⇨ Pardon the winners (and, of course, the losers will no longer cause a problem).

Outrageous. No one would EVER propose such a thing today.
    But in history? Yes.
    In the Wild West days of gunfighters … the Earps and the cowboys at OK Corral, perhaps? But in Britain?
    Yes. Scotland, in fact. In 1396, not only was a gang fight to the death condoned by King Robert III, but he went along to watch clansmen butcher one another.

### Broadswords and butchery

> In those days there was no law in Scotland, but the strong oppressed the weak, and the whole kingdom was one den of thieves. Homicides, robberies, fire-raisings, and other misdeeds remained unpunished, and justice seemed banished beyond the kingdom's bounds.
>
>                     The *Chartularium Episcopatus Moraviensis*,
>                     written at Elgin Cathedral for the year 1398

Robert III (1337–1406) may have been king in name, but the Scottish peasants under the feudal system were more controlled by the people immediately above them on the pyramid of power – their clan chiefs.

While the clan system offered kinship, identity, food and livelihood, it also created a ready supply of peasants willing to fight for their chief. The Norman lords in England were united in their need to keep their Saxon peasants oppressed. It didn't make sense to scrap among themselves.

Scotland was different. Norman Scotland was 'one nation' in name only. If the chiefs were feuding, then the kingdom fell into anarchy and the king himself interfered at his peril. And Robert III was no 'Braveheart'. He even described himself as 'the worst of kings and the most miserable of men'.

So, it is no surprise that rotten Robert came up with the idea of sanctioning a lethal contest between two of his clans.

### Clan clash

What was the fight about? About 'honour'. The combatants were at war over which group got to take the right flank when the national army went to war ... usually against England. The warriors on the right wing held the position of the highest honour.

Honour? No, that is not an outdated ideal of a Norman knight. It has resonated through history.

> *Never give in – never, never, never, never, in nothing great or small, large or petty, never give in except to convictions of honour and good sense.*
> Winston Churchill (1874 – 1965), British politician and writer

The details are vague – and the combative clans disputed – but the majority view is that it was a feud between the Kay and the Chattan clans. Or maybe it was an internal family affair of Clan Chattan – a collection of clans that included Macphersons, Davidsons, Keiths and Macintoshes.

Whoever was fighting, the set-up seems clear:

⇨ Each clan was to choose thirty men (again, number disputed).
⇨ They must decide their differences by the sword, without being allowed any other weapon.
⇨ The conquered clan were to be pardoned for all their former offences.[5]
⇨ The conquerors would be honoured with the royal favour – fighting on the right hand of 'the worst of kings'.

On a Monday morning in late September, the clans marched through the streets of Perth, accompanied by bagpipes and armed with bows and arrows, swords, shields, knives and axes. They marched to the western banks of the river Tay.

Barriers were erected on three sides of the North Inch, to keep spectators off the pitch, the river Tay forming the natural fourth barrier to the north. It was a gladiatorial amphitheatre or a corral.[6] The Gilded Arbour summerhouse of the Dominican Friary was adapted into a grandstand for the king and his court.

The peasant spectators had to make do with benches where they could sit and munch on porridge sandwiches as they watched men die.

His Majesty himself sat as judge. Crowds gathered, and the fighters appeared, but just as they were ready to engage, one of the Chattan clansmen withdrew from fear (and who amongst

---

5. As 'conquered' on this occasion included the fighters – and as the defeated fighters would be dead – it must have been a great consolation that as your opponent thrust his sword into you, you fell bleeding to the earth with the joy of knowing you'd been 'pardoned'. It must be a bit like dying as a Catholic with a priest pattering out his hasty orisons.
6. Given the names of the rival sides, you might think that a writer would suggest it was the 'Oh. Kay Corral.' You might think that; I couldn't possibly comment.

us can blame him?). Some sources say he threw a sickie. The Kays offered no help, so the king demanded that one of the other side should be withdrawn, so as to even up the contest. The Kay fighters – obviously wired up to the eyeballs – were not having that. One of the spectators presented himself before the king and offered his services, which were accepted.

The resulting fight was so bloody and furious that the king and spectators were seized with 'an inexpressible horror'.

> *Dismembered knight: 'I'm the Black Knight. I'm invincible.'*
> *Enemy: 'You're a loony. What you gonna do, bleed on me?'*
> Monty Python and the Holy Grail

Only one Kay survived, saving himself by swimming the river Tay – the exhausted Chattans were in no condition to prevent him. This battle didn't defuse the rivalry, it simply postponed it for a few years (because the best and strongest warriors of each clan had been killed).

Far from seeing it as a stain on the history of Scotland, the great novelist Sir Walter Scott described it in gleeful detail:

> *Blood flowed fast, and the groans of those who fell began to mingle with the cries of those who fought. The wild notes of the pipes were still heard above the tumult and stimulated to further exertion the fury of the combatants.*
>
> *At once, however, as if by mutual agreement, the instruments sounded a retreat. The two parties disengaged themselves from each other to take breath for a few minutes. About twenty of both sides lay on the field, dead or dying; arms and legs lopped off, heads cleft to the chin, slashes deep through the shoulder to the breast, showed at once the fury of the combat, the ghastly character of the weapons used, and the fatal strength of the arms which wielded them.*
> Sir Walter Scott (1771–1832),
> Scottish historical novelist, in *The Fair Maid of Perth*

On a worldwide stage of atrocities, the Battle of North Inch wasn't significant in itself, but it did set a precedent for clan rivalries being 'sorted' by murder and retaliation. One hundred and eighty years later came the Battle of the Spoiling of the Dyke …

## Brawling

*BRAWL: Middle English braule, brall, 'brawl, squabble' from braulen, brallen 'to clamour, boast, quarrel'.*

Dictionary

The source of the crime of 'brawling' probably isn't what you imagine. For 'brawling', in law, was the offence of 'quarrelling, or creating a disturbance in a church or churchyard'. The law against brawling was covered in church courts until 1860, but hardly ever used, and abolished in 1967.

Mary Tudor's government made brawling illegal in 1551 with an Act of Parliament, and the punishment? Stay in jail until you repent.

*If any person shall, by words only, quarrel, chide or brawl in any church or churchyard, it shall be lawful for the ordinary of the place where the same shall be done and proved by two lawful witnesses, to suspend any person so offending.*

1551 Act of Parliament

If brawling is restricted to church property, then some revolting peasants of Western Scotland should have been made to repent till Judgement Day. Their crime was hideous.

In 1578, the Macleods of Waternish and the Macdonalds of Uist were at one another's throats – and sporrans – on the Isle of Skye.

The spark that lit this fiery feud was probably struck in 1577. It's said that a group of Macleods landed on the Macdonalds' island of Eigg. The Macdonalds hid in a cave but the marauding Macleods spotted a careless Macdonald face. The Macleods piled thatch and roof timbers at the cave entrance and set fire to it. They took care to dampen the flames with water, so that the cave was filled with smoke, and asphyxiated everyone inside. Some 395 Macdonalds died. One old woman – who had found an alternative hiding place – survived. (Why is there *always* one survivor?)

The following year the Macleods were attending a St Conan's Church service at Trumpan on Skye when the Macdonalds arrived. They'd landed in a fleet of eight ships at Ardmore Bay with murder in mind. They surrounded the church and set it on fire. Brawling? Or arson?

*Give a man a fire and he's warm for the day. But set fire to him and he's warm for the rest of his life.*
Terry Pratchett (1948 – 2015), English author of fantasy novels

Bagpipes played to drown out the screams as the worshippers died. All the unarmed and defenceless Macleods inside were burned alive apart from one slender girl. She slipped through the narrow slit window at one end of the church and escaped unseen in the billowing smoke. Though she took fatal injuries in her escape, the girl ran to fetch help from the chief of Clan Macleod at Dunvegan.[7] (Yet again, a lone survivor. This one ran *10 miles* with her fatal injuries. Some athlete.)

---

7. Another version of the tale says a local fisherman saw the Macdonald armada on its way and sailed to Dunvegan to alert the chief. By the time the Macleods had donned their dirks, collected their claymores and polished off their porridge they were too late to save the church but in time to intercept the raiders.

The rest of the Macleod clan were alerted by the smoke and the fire. They ran to the church, armed and looking for vengeance.

*Before the Macdonalds could regain their boats, which by the receding of the tide, were high and dry upon the rocks at Ardmore, they were attacked by the Macleods. A desperate struggle ensued in which all the Macdonalds were slain.*

Alexander Cameron,
*The History and Traditions of Skye*, 1892

One account says that the Macleods unfurled the clan's magical Fairy Flag, and their numbers were instantly doubled. Some readers – especially those who like Macdonalds – may view this as 'cheating' and 'not cricket'. But don't feel tempted to launch a retaliatory attack. You see, this was the second unveiling of the Fairy Flag, and it can be used three times before losing its power. The Macleods of Skye still have another in their locker. Be warned.

The Macdonalds tried to retreat to their boats on the shore, only to find they had been stranded high and dry by the retreating tide. The invaders were slaughtered ... though some say a single boat escaped and carried the bad news back to Uist.[8]

As for the corpses of the slain Macdonalds ...

*Their bodies were range in line alongside a turf dyke, and the dyke was tumbled over on the top of them – a quick but unfeeling form of burial.*

Alexander Cameron,
*The History and Traditions of Skye*, 1892

---

8. Again, there is an unreliable alternative version, which says that a storm came up and wrecked the boat, so *not one* of the Macdonalds survived the day.

This rough burial under a wall of stone and turf gave the incident its populist name, the Battle of the Spoiling Dyke. It is also known as the Battle of Waternish. Years later, visitors reported seeing bones protruding from the mass grave.

That's a lazy and disrespectful way to treat an enemy's corpse ... which is probably what the Macleods intended.

It's hard to feel sorry for the Macdonalds, who started it, and who slew helpless Macleods when they were in church. And having frazzled the Macleods, why didn't they make their escape? The girl had to run 10 miles for help and the armed response unit had to run 10 miles back in battle gear. Three hours in total? What were the Macdonald raiders *doing* in all that time, we have to ask? Did they have chestnuts roasting on the open fire?

> *Procrastination is opportunity's assassin.*
> Victor Kiam (1926 – 2001),
> American entrepreneur

The ruthless raiders left the roofless ruins of St Conan's Church, which can still be seen today. Drive to Skye and you'll find it at the end of the road ... as it was for those Macdonalds.

## Gang violence

> *People love stories about the Mafia: 'The Godfather', 'American Gangster'.*
> Jason Statham (b. 1967), English actor and former model

True, but remember ...

> *The classy gangster is a Hollywood invention.*
> Orson Welles (1915 – 1985), American actor,
> director, writer and producer in theatre, radio and film

24

The classy gangster is indeed a Hollywood invention. Orson Welles was probably thinking of films like *Angels with Dirty Faces*. The gangster (played by James Cagney) is loved by the local street kids – the eponymous angels. He is sentenced to the electric chair. Will his gangsterism be elevated to martyrdom in the eyes of the innocent 'angels'? Will they try to emulate his criminal lifestyle?

A childhood friend of Cagney, played by Pat O'Brien, asks him for an electric-chair favour. Will he go to the chair a drivelling coward so the kids don't see him as an heroic 'victim'? What does James Cagney do? (This is hardly a 'spoiler' for those who haven't seen the picture because it is the bleedin' obvious.) He goes down screaming as his old friend asks. Yes, a 'classy gangster'.

From earliest historical records gangsters have been thugs and bullies.

### Roxton ravaging

Castles have stone walls and (until cannon were invented) they were easy to defend. In time it became enshrined in law:

> *For a man's house is his castle, and each man's home is his safest refuge.*
>
> Sir Edward Coke (1552–1634), English barrister and judge,
> *The Institutes of the Laws of England*, 1628

And the home didn't have to be a substantial house, according to a British Prime Minister …

> *The poorest man may in his cottage bid defiance to all the forces of the Crown. It may be frail – its roof may shake – the wind may blow through it – the storm may enter – the rain may enter – but the King of England cannot enter.*
>
> William Pitt the Elder (1708–1778),
> British Prime Minister

But gangsters down the years have proved that walls are *not* as strong as words. The English man and English woman's homes are NOT their castles and never were. The walls of wattle and daub (or straw and mud) would resist the blowing of a Big Bad Wolf but not the battering of hefty men.

In 1269, the village of Roxton was shattered by a savage attack by a robber gang that left four dead and three seriously injured. This gang of armed thugs burst clear through the walls of Ralph Bovetoun's house and robbed it as two girls who'd been staying there fled.

The people in the next house were not so lucky. Maude del Forde and Alice Pressade were in bed when the gang broke in. Maude was struck on the head with an axe to stop her screams being heard. Witnesses have described seeing her brains spilling out onto the pillow. Alice died later from the wounds they gave her.

John Cobbler's house was attacked on two sides, with window shutters torn down and the door smashed in. The man was taken outside and killed. His wife, Alma, and daughter Agnes suffered axe wounds to their heads and knife wounds to the chest and arms. Their other daughter managed to hide between a chest and a basket.

Alma Cobbler was able to describe her attackers before she died.

The twist in the tale? This was no gang of peasants out to make a quick groat. They were tax collectors from the local monastery.

The Sheriff of Bedfordshire told worried village peasants that these evil men would be caught and executed. Hanging a bunch of tax men? That must have been a popular public event.

## Wild Wales

In the 1550s, the Red Bandits of Mawddwy brought terror to mid-Wales for ten years, stealing sheep and cattle in the Dinas Mawddwy region. They attacked anyone travelling through the area. They are believed to have taken their name from their distinctive copper-coloured hair. This was no little street-corner gang. This was a small army.

Sir John Wynn of Gwydir rounded up their leaders and eighty of them were sentenced to death by Baron Owen. They used to meet in Mallwyd at the Brigands Inn and they were buried on Rhos Goch, the Red Moor, just 2 miles away.

One Red Bandit mother screamed at the judge:

*I curse you. One day my children's hands will be washed in your blood.*

Sure enough, on 11 October 1555, Judge Lewis Owen was on his way to his home at Dolgellau when he was stopped at Dugoed Mawddwy by the remnants of the robber family. The judge was shot with thirty arrows. They weren't messing about.

Then they carved up the corpse and washed their hands in the judge's blood, just to fulfil granny's prediction. They, in turn, were executed, and why not? They'd been caught red-handed.

## Heroic housebreakers

The idea of robbers as gentlemen of the road persists. Dick Turpin is one ghostly gangster whose aura of polite pilferer persists against all the evidence.

Dick Turpin (who also called himself John Palmer) was born in 1705 and hanged in 1739. Thereafter the romantic legend grew that:

⇨ He was a brave and handsome hero who was a wonderful rider.
⇨ He robbed stagecoaches but was always very polite ... especially to ladies.
⇨ He rode his gallant horse, Black Bess, all the way from Essex to York in record time to prove he couldn't have committed a crime ... though he had.

All part of the legend and all mistaken. The truth is, Turpin was as far from being a gentleman as London was from York.

The Essex boy followed his father to be a butcher boy – buy animals, cut them up and sell the meat for a small profit. Obviously the less you pay for the dead animal the greater your profit. And if that animal was stolen you were on to a winner. That would be how he fell in with the Essex Gang.

They were deer thieves in the early 1730s. In 1723, the Black Act outlawed the blackening or disguising of faces while in the forests. The aim of the law was to make the apprehension of poachers easier. By 1737, the penalty of seven years' transportation was introduced for any man trying to disguise himself.

It didn't deter the poachers, and they took to threatening gamekeepers and their families to stay ahead of the law. They stole the deer, butcher-boy Turpin disposed of the animals.

Then he discovered it was as easy to simply join the Essex Gang. But the authorities were clamping down on poaching deer so the Essex Gang diversified. They became a crew of violent housebreakers. They entered someone's home by kicking down the door, the way the Roxton rabble kicked down walls. They searched the house and if they found nothing worthwhile they tortured the occupants till they revealed any valuables. At one isolated farm they roasted an old farmer's wife over her own fire till she told them where her money was hidden.

In 1734, Turpin and five other men raided the home of Ambrose Skinner, a 73-year-old farmer from Barking, and rode off with £300. A cool £10,000 each at today's values.

*The only point in making money is, you can tell some big shot where to go.*

Humphrey Bogart (1899 – 1957),
American screen and stage actor, and cultural icon

You can see Bogart's point. Money gives a disadvantaged lad like Turpin the power to hold his peasant head up among the big shots of the world.

The gang grew more violent and more prolific. They attacked a 70-year-old farmer named Lawrence. They pulled his trousers around his ankles, and dragged him around the house, but the old man refused to tell them where he'd hidden his money. Turpin beat Lawrence's bare buttocks with his pistols while other members of the gang beat him around the head with their pistols.

They emptied a kettle of hot water over his head, then forced him to sit bare-buttocked on the fire, and pulled him around the house by his nose, and hair. A gang member, Gregory, took one of the maidservants upstairs and raped her. The gang escaped with a haul of less than £30.

But crime (according to the cliché) doesn't pay ... or not for an extended period. Many of the gang were arrested. One betrayed the others and Turpin was targeted. The handsome robber? No ...

*Richard Turpin, a butcher by trade, is a tall fresh coloured man, very much marked with the small pox, about 26 years of age, about five feet nine inches high, wears a blue grey coat and a natural wig.*

*The London Gazette*, 1834

Not that handsome then. Turpin was a wanted man. Time for another career change.

He became a highwayman. Turpin armed himself, stopped a gentleman on the road and threatened him with a pistol. In fact, the man was the famous highwayman Tom King. King took the attempted robbery in a good spirit and adopted young Turpin as a partner. They spent two years terrorising the Essex roads. When King was caught Turpin tried to rescue him.

> *King cried out, 'Dick, shoot him, or we are taken by God,' at which Instant Turpin fired his Pistol, and it mist Mr. Bayes, and shot King in two Places, who cried out, 'Dick, you have killed me'; which Turpin hearing, he rode away as hard as he could.*
>
> Report by Richard Bayes, landlord of the
> Green Man public house, 1739

Turpin 'accidentally' shot Tom King dead ... maybe.[9]

Turpin rode away to concealment in Epping Forest. This time he didn't threaten the gamekeeper who came across him ...

> *Richard Turpin did on Wednesday the 4th of May last, barbarously murdered Thomas Morris, Servant to Henry Tomson, one of the Keepers of Epping-Forest.*
>
> *The Gentleman's Magazine*, 1737

---

9. Some have suggested Turpin aimed to shoot King so he wouldn't be betrayed ... and would get to keep their earnings. Would Turpin – a man who roasts old ladies – have qualms about silencing his mentor and partner that way? The report went on: 'King fell at the Shot, though he lived a Week after, and gave Turpin the Character of a Coward.' Accident? Or the murder of a mate? Make up your own mind, members of the jury.

This cold-blooded murder raised the reward on Turpin to £200. Another move would be good for the health of his neck, so he went to Lincolnshire and Yorkshire and changed his name to John Palmer, horse dealer.

### Literary legend

Of course Turpin did not ride from London to York overnight on Black Bess. That was an episode recorded by Daniel Defoe, in his 1727 work *A tour Thro' the Whole Island of Great Britain*. After a robbery in Kent in 1676, William Nevison was said to have ridden to York to establish an alibi. Defoe's account of that journey became part of folk legend.

But to return to John Palmer. His end was ignominious, not heroic. In 1738, Turpin shot another man's game cock in the street. He was arrested and shut in York Castle ... for heroically and drunkenly shooting a chicken.

Turpin sent a letter to his brother-in-law appealing for help. The relative refused to pay the postage and the handwriting was recognised by Turpin's old school teacher, who went to York to identify Palmer and the murderous Turpin.

On his way to his execution at the place now (ironically) York horse-racing course, the legend of the gallant hero began to build. Turpin bought a new frock coat and shoes, and looked nonchalant as he was taken through York by open cart to the gallows.

Reports said Turpin 'behav'd himself with amazing assurance', and 'bow'd to the spectators as he passed'. He climbed a ladder to the gallows and *The Gentleman's Magazine* reported Turpin's brashness:

> *Turpin behaved in an undaunted manner; as he mounted the ladder, feeling his right leg tremble, he spoke a few words to the topsman, then threw himself off, and expir'd in five minutes.*

A brave death sent a melancholic mist over the murderous life. But it was a hundred years later when the lies and reimagining of Turpin's life really began. The novelist William Harrison Ainsworth (1805–1882) wrote the most unutterable drivel about Turpin's life. Ainsworth 'almost regrets' the demise of the highwayman. Really? Maybe Mr Ainsworth was never robbed or had his backside held over an open fire by the hoodlum.

But it is the drivel that has been remembered.

*Rash daring was the main feature of Turpin's character. Like our great Nelson, he knew fear only by name;*

*Turpin was the ultimus Romanorum, the last of a race, which – we were almost about to say we regret – is now altogether extinct.*

*Several successors he had, it is true, but no name worthy to be recorded after his own.*

*With him expired the chivalrous spirit which animated successively the bosoms of so many knights of the road.*

*With him died away that passionate love of enterprise, that high spirit of devotion to the fair sex, which was extinguished at last by the cord that tied the heroic Turpin to the remorseless tree.*

William Harrison Ainsworth, *Rookwood*, 1834

The highwayman villain Dick Turpin was buried in St George's churchyard in the city. He was dug up and buried in a doctor's garden till the doctor could start dissecting the corpse. But before the doctor could so much as sharpen his scalpel, Turpin's friends dug the body up again and buried it in the churchyard a second time. This time they poured quicklime over the body to destroy it.

Rest in pieces, Dick.

# Chapter 2

# Mediaeval Misery

*The infectiousness of crime is like that of the plague.*
Napoleon Bonaparte (1769–1821),
Corsican military leader and French statesman

Peasants were at the bottom of the feudal system pyramid. And if you were at the bottom of a pyramid you'd be crushed. As if that weren't enough, your evil lord made you work like a slave labourer; meanwhile, your Good Lord sent you something to help relieve your misery. He sent you plagues.

## Shoplifting

*I have kleptomania. But when it gets bad, I take something for it.*
Ken Dodd (1927–2018), English comedian and singer

Shoplifting: to career criminals, known as 'the five-finger discount'. To shopkeepers, written off as 'shrinkage'.

In 2018 there were 200 thefts an hour reported from convenience stores of Britain alone. That's shrinkage of ice-caps-in-global-warming proportions.

It's seen by some as a trivial crime, but it's the sort of little-acorn crime from which whacking great oak-tree offences can grow. Lizzie Borden (1860–1927) was an American woman who gained infamy after being tried (and acquitted) for the 1892

axe murders of her parents (but everyone knows whodunit …
and it wasn't fairies at the bottom of her garden).

Lizzie was accused of shoplifting, though that paled in
comparison with the more infamous crime of which (repeat
after me) she was *innocent*.

As she was so very innocent you must disregard the jingle

> *Lizzie Borden took an axe*
> *And gave her mother forty whacks.*
> *When she saw what she had done,*
> *She gave her father forty-one.*

Jean Genet (1910–1986) began his criminal life as a French
shoplifter … and really went bad when he turned to writing novels.

Those caught stealing less than £200 are now dealt with by post
these days.[1] How different to the fate of mediaeval miscreants.
A law known as the Gibbet Law gave the Lord of the Manor for
Halifax the power to condemn someone to death by the Halifax
Gibbet if they were found guilty of stealing something that was
worth more than 13p.

> *The inhabitants of the forest of Hardwick (which was co-*
> *extensive with the Parish of Halifax) had the custom, that, if*
> *a felon was taken within their liberty with goods stolen out or*
> *within the liberty of the said forest, to the value of thirteenpence*
> *halfpenny, he should, after three markets, or meeting days,*
> *within the Town of Halifax, be tried, and being condemned,*
> *be taken to the Gibbet, and have his head cut off from his body.*
>
> Halifax Gibbet Law, *The County Words*, 1870

---

1. Smart shoplifters know this, so go from shop to shop pinching up to £199
   worth of goods then moving on. And, no, this is not a textbook treatise on
   how to get away with such antisocial behaviour. Don't do it.

The first recorded use of the Halifax Gibbet was in 1286, when John of Dalton was executed.

### The running man

> *From Hull, Halifax, and Hell, good Lord deliver us.*
>
> Yorkshire proverb

The saying is based on the belief among beggars that Hull and Halifax were the two towns in the north where you got the harshest punishment from the magistrates for breaking the law.

In Hull you got a good whipping. But in Halifax in the Middle Ages you suffered much worse. Much, much worse.

> *The town's named Kingston, Hull's the furious river;*
> *And from Halifax's dangers, I say, Lord, deliver.*
> *At Halifax, the law so sharp doth deal,*
> *That whoso more than 13 pence doth steal;*
> *They have a gyn² that wondrous, quick and well,*
> *Sends thieves all headless unto Heaven or Hell.*
>
> Anonymous poem, 1709

Yes, a machine for slicing off heads built in a Yorkshire town 600 years before Doctor Joseph-Ignace Guillotin gave his name to the French terror topper. Doc Guillotin may have *proposed* a decapitation machine, but it was in order to spare aristocrats the bungling headsman and peasants the strangling hangman. Its aim was to end life, not inflict pain. It was to be capital punishment for all, regardless of class. *Égalité.*

---

2. Short for 'engine', but engine wouldn't scan.

Joseph-Ignace was mortified that the government ordered such machines to be made in his name, though he was on the committee that commissioned a prototype. Many alternatives have been invented down the years – how about 'The National Razor' or 'The Regretful Climb' anyone?

But the 'guillotine' name stuck (unlike the victims' heads). The prototype was built by a German whose day job was making harpsichords. The Guillotin family felt obliged to change their name.

A man named Guillotin was executed by the guillotine – he was a doctor from Lyons, but it gave rise to the neat urban myth that the inventor of the guillotine died on his own invention. He didn't. Joseph-Ignace died of natural causes.

But where did Guillotin get the idea for his slicing device? From (among other sources) the Halifax Gibbet.

*Halifax horror*

The machine consisted of an axe head weighted with a heavy wooden block that ran in grooves between two 4 metre uprights, a rope over a pulley, allowing it to be raised and held at the top with a pin. When the pin was pulled out the axe fell once the prisoner was in place.

Around a hundred people were beheaded in Halifax between the first recorded execution in 1286 and the last in 1650. By 1650, public opinion considered beheading to be a rather excessive punishment for petty theft; use of the Halifax Gibbet was forbidden by Oliver Cromwell. (A non-working replica was erected on the site in 1974.)

If people caught stealing less than £200 today are treated leniently, then the cut-off point in Halifax was 13 pence. Steal anything worth 12p or less and you were punished but not beheaded.

The writer Daniel Defoe said that the gibbet was used for *any* 13p felons, but the Halifax folk told him it was really there to protect the produce of the local cloth weavers ... obviously a vengeful bunch.

Oh, what satisfaction they must have taken to see thieves of their cloth perish under a blade that ...

*doth fall down with such violence, that if the neck of the transgressor were so big as that of a bull, it should be cut in sunder at a stroke, and roll from the body by an huge distance.*

Raphael Holinshed (1529–1580), English Chronicler, *An Historicall Description of the Iland of Britaine*[3]

There is a story that a Halifax market-woman was riding her horse past the Gibbet as the axe fell and the severed head bounced across the platform and into her lap, where it seized her apron in its teeth and refused to let go.

There doesn't appear to have been a formal 'executioner' appointed and no one seems to have wanted the responsibility for finishing off the felon. So, it became a custom to attach a rope to the holding pin and fasten the other end to an animal – a cow from the market or a horse. When the animal moved, the pin was pulled, the blade dropped, and the victim died.

Who killed the thief? No one.

Another legend said that if a condemned prisoner escaped on the day of his/her execution – or snatched his head away between the pin being pulled and the axe hitting the block – then s/he would be freed. They only had to run 450 metres and cross the town's boundary, Hebble Brook.

---

3. Holinshead famously provided source material for Shakespeare plays like *Macbeth*. You can see where the Bard acquired his habit of dodgy spelling.

The peasant pilferer John Lacey, on 29 January 1623, did escape on the day of his execution. He remained in exile for seven years before returning. It seems he believed that crossing Hebble Brook constituted a 'reprieve' and that his seven years' 'exile' was a statutory period. It wasn't.

Lacey returned, was recognised, arrested and executed on the Gibbet. Lifting shopper suffered chopper.

The public house The Running Man celebrates Lacey's temporary reprieve.

## Revolt

### Peasants' revolt

> *Revolutions are the locomotives of history.*
>
> Karl Marx (1818 – 1883), economist,
> political theorist and revolutionary socialist[4]

> *Those are my principles, and if you don't like them … well, I have others.*
>
> Groucho Marx (1890 – 1977), American comedian

There are times when the suffering becomes too much and the peasants revolt. The last straw does not break the camel's back – it's the accumulated weight of all the other straws. If the feudal system was a pyramid, then there's an awful lot of weight bearing down on the bottom layer.

And so it was with THE Peasants' Revolt of 1381.

The idiot's guide to history has simplified it to say the Poll Tax was the spark that lit the powder keg. But, as you aren't an idiot, you will appreciate that it is never that simple.

---

4. Though, as he himself said, 'If anything is certain, it is that I myself am not a Marxist.' Hmm. A thought-provoking paradox or a lame-brain thing to say?

*The tree of liberty must be refreshed from time to time with the blood of patriots and tyrants.*

Thomas Jefferson (1743 – 1826), American Foundling Father, principal author of the Declaration of Independence, and 3rd President of the US

We can guess President Jeff was hoping there would be more tyrant blood on the floor than patriot blood. But he is clearly from the same school as the Roman poet Horace, with his '*Dulce et decorum est*'. The idea that 'It is sweet and fitting to die for one's country' was pretty comprehensively dismantled as 'the old lie' by Wilfred Owen in his poem 'Dulce et Decorum Est'. And we have to trust Owen's judgement because he saw the blood of patriots in close up.[5]

The peasants were prepared to water the tree of their liberty with blue blood. Priest John Ball told the rebels:

*Now is the time.*

John Ball (1338 – 1381),
radical English priest

The leader of the rebels was Wat Tyler (who may well have been a tiler – roofs, not bathrooms and kitchens). As the march neared London, Wat boasted:

*In four days' time all the laws of England shall be coming from my mouth.*

Wat Tyler, (d. 1381)

---

5. On 4 November 1918, just one week before the armistice was declared, Wilfred Owen was killed in action during a British assault on the German-held Sambre Canal. Neither sweet nor fitting for his loved ones. A tragedy for them and a loss to us all of the inspirational poems he never wrote.

What did Wat's peasants do? They:

⇨ broke into Marshalsea and Fleet prisons and set the prisoners free.
⇨ ransacked lawyers' chambers and burned all the papers they could find.
⇨ plundered Lambeth Palace – residence of the Lord Chancellor – and burned down the estate of St John's Prior.
⇨ entered the palace of the king's uncle, John of Gaunt, and threw his valuables into the Thames ... while leaving the servants unharmed.

Richard II said he was sympathetic to the rebels. Wat Tyler believed him. Wat a mistake. The king went down the Thames on a barge to meet them but retreated when he heard their new and alarming demands: Richard was told he must have his top fifteen advisers beheaded as traitors.

From the Tower he had a proclamation read. It said the young king would pardon the rebels if they went home and wrote him a letter with their grievances. That only poured paraffin on the flames. They now wanted the heads of:

*all the men of the Chancery and the exchequer and everyone who could write a writ or a letter.*

They also demanded they meet the king in person at Mile End ...

*a fair, plain place where the people of the city did sport them in the summer season.*

### Meanwhile, back at the Tower

As Wat Tyler negotiated, a fearsome woman of Kent, Johanna Ferrour, led an assault on the Tower, where their main targets were cowering – the Chancellor/Archbishop of Canterbury (Simon Sudbury) and Treasurer (Robert Hales).[6]

In court documents she was described as:

*Chief perpetrator and leader of rebellious evildoers from Kent.*

She was also accused of burning the Savoy Palace – the grandest house in London at the time – and stealing a chest of gold.

There were guards at the Tower, but clearly not sturdy beef eaters because they simply opened the gates and let Johanna and friends in. (Or did they? Some say Richard told the guards to let them in so Sudbury and Hales would be sacrificial scapegoats and save him having to give them a trial.)

*and at last found the Archbishop of Canterbury, called Simon, a valiant man and a wise, and chief chancellor of England, and a little before he had said mass before the king. These gluttons took him and strake off his head, and also, they beheaded the lord of Saint John's and a friar minor, master in medicine, they slew him in despite of his master, and a sergeant at arms called John Leg;*[7]

The Archbishop had his head forced onto an executioner's block. It took eight blows to hack through his neck. Clearly the peasants hadn't had a lot of practice at the decapitation lark. That must have hurt. His mitre was then nailed to his head ... which wouldn't hurt at all.

---

6. Hales was hated as the tax collector in chief. If you are looking for a model of understatement then the chronicler Walsingham Hales was a 'magnanimous knight, though the commons loved him not'.
7. Sir John Legge, the king's tax collector for Kent. Sergeant at *arms* called *Leg*? Once the Tower fell he was out on a limb.

*And these four heads were set on four long spears and they made them to be borne before them through the streets of London and at last set them a-high on London bridge, as though they had been traitors to the king and to the realm.*

His head was stuck on London Bridge (and for the ghouls among you, that head can still be seen at the church of St Gregory at Sudbury in Suffolk. As Archbishop of Canterbury his noodle could literally be seen as head of the church.)

Hales's head joined Sudbury's. As treasurer, he took a large portion of the blame for the introduction of the Poll Tax. That was a bit unfair as the taxes had been passed shortly before Hales became treasurer. But no one worried about fairness.

On 15 June 1381, along with Mayor Walworth, Richard II rode out to meet Wat and his peasant followers.

Tyler made his demands. The principal demand was an end to serfdom – a dismantling of the feudal system. The people of England should be free to buy or rent their own land, buy and sell their own goods, and have the right to take their grievances, gripes and grumbles to the king's court.

They repeated the call for the execution of their oppressors whilst the rebels themselves would be granted an amnesty. Richard was equivocal about the executions – the alleged traitors would have fair trials. But apart from that he appeared to cave in to their ultimatums.

*To this the King gave an easy answer and said that he should have all that he could fairly grant, reserving only for himself the regality of his crown. And then he bade him go back to his home, without making further delay.*

*Anonimalle Chronicle* – mediaeval sourcebook

An unlikely victory was on the cards.

*Spitting mad*

At Mile End, Wat was getting carried away with the feeling of power. He made further demands: the end of tithes, the abolition of bishops, the redistribution of wealth, equality before the law, and the freedom to kill the animals in the forest.

But Wat's boorish arrogance was the undoing of him and the cause. He called for a bottle of water …

> *because of the great heat that he was in and he rinsed his mouth in a very rude and disgusting fashion before the King's face.*

A servant of the king, Sir John Newton, was disgusted and called Wat:

> *the greatest thief and robber in all Kent.*

Tyler made to attack Newton but was held back and arrested by the Lord Mayor of London, William Walworth. Wat lost the plot and tried to stab the mayor. A pointless stab since the mayor was wearing armour. Sensible precaution. The mayor drew his sword and struck Wat Tyler.

> *He gave him a deep cut on the neck, and then a great cut on the head. And during this scuffle one of the King's household drew his sword and ran Watt two or three times through the body, mortally wounding him. And he spurred his horse, crying to the commons to avenge him, and the horse carried him some four score paces, and then he fell to the ground, half dead.*

Half-dead soon became full-dead.

*When the commons saw that their chieftain, Watt Tyler, was
dead in such a manner, they fell to the ground there among the
wheat, like beaten men, imploring the King for mercy for their
misdeeds.*

He was dragged away by his friends to a hospital for the poor.
There his corpse was tracked down by the mayor, hauled back to
Smithfield, and publicly decapitated.

Mayor Walworth knew what all rebel-crushers knew: it's
not enough to kill the revolting peasant; you have to make a
revolting spectacle of it. *Pour encourage les autres.*[8] Tyler's head
was stuck on a pole, carried through the city, and displayed on
London Bridge.[9]

The peasants were – like Wat Tyler – left without a head and
melted back to the misery of their hovels.

Richard II had made concessions to the rebels, of course,
but he withdrew them all. Not satisfied with Wat's head, the
authorities hunted down and executed other leading figures,
like the priest John Ball. Revolt over.

So why did the rebels risk – and in many case lose – their lives?

*The face of evil is always the face of need.*
William S. Burroughs (1914 – 1997),
American novelist

The desperate rebels saw a weakness in the rule of England.
King Richard II came to the throne at the age of ten. After the

---

8. A phrase deriving from Voltaire's novel *Candide* about the execution of
Admiral Byng. *'Dans ce pays-ci, il est bon de tuer de temps en temps un
amiral pour encourager les autres,'* or 'In this country, it is wise to kill an
admiral from time to time to encourage the others.'

9. It has been suggested the head was held in place with pole tacks, but I would
never repeat such a tasteless joke.

ruthless rule of Edward III, here was a new, green monarch, easy to overthrow. If the peasants were footballers, then they saw Richard as an open goal.

The spark to the tinder was the Poll Tax. But the real grievance was the bonds of villeinage and the lack of legal and political rights.

Once the pimply boy-king Richard had defeated the rebels he withdrew his promises of freedom and there was certainly little in the way of a pardon. During the following weeks an estimated 1,500 rebels were executed. Now he was safe, we saw the true face of royalty when Richard told a group of peasants at Walthamstow:

*You wretches, detestable on land and sea; you who seek equality with lords are unworthy to live. Give this message to your colleagues. Villeins you were and Villeins you are still: For as long as we live we will strive to suppress you, and your misery will be an example in the eyes of posterity. However, we will spare your lives if you remain faithful. Choose now which you want to follow.*

*Aftermath*

Serfdom, not Poll Tax, was at the heart of the disaffection. Record numbers were being fined for the 'crime' of finding work elsewhere. Those who were permitted still had to return to help with their lord's harvest.

The peasant even had to pay a fee to marry the woman of his choice. Richard had told the Walthamstow peasants:

*You will remain in bondage, not as before, but incomparably harsher.*

Rich was wrong. The revolt *did* mark the beginning of the end of serfdom in mediaeval England, and a change in feudalism. Wat Tyler started the process, but it was slow. Other revolts were needed.

The Jack Cade rebellion ended with his execution in 1450.

In 1549 it was East Anglian Robert Kett's turn to lead a march on London. Serfdom was still an issue. One of Kett's demands was:

*All bond me may be free, for God made all free with his precious blood shedding.*

As you'd guess, it was Kett's blood that was shed under the oppressor's axe.

But it was another step along the road to peasant freedom. The peasants' revolts were criminal acts of murder and destruction in the name of liberty, self-determination and equality.

## War crimes

*Humankind seems to have an enormous capacity for savagery, for brutality, for lack of empathy, for lack of compassion.*
                    Annie Lennox (b. 1954), Scottish singer,
                            songwriter and political activist

Mediaeval wars brought out the worst in some of the peasants, both men and women. In the 1400s, despite the best efforts of Wat Tyler and his revolting mates, peasants were still liable to be 'called up' by their lords to serve in English wars. Archery, as a village hobby, was encouraged so the menfolk would be ready to serve.

The lords rode on horses in armour while the peasants – the ones who suffered the diseases on the marches – trudged behind until the battle. Then the archers went to the front. Cannon fodder.

### Sisters are doing it for themselves

Richard II had defeated the Peasants' Revolt, but he couldn't defeat his own enemies within. In 1399, Henry Bolinbroke took the throne and had himself proclaimed Henry IV.

Richard allegedly starved to death. He had been created Prince of Wales in 1376 and enlisted large numbers of Welsh troops who served him loyally. Richard had been popular in Wales. His enemy, Henry IV, by default, wasn't.

At the end of the 1390s, prophets in Wales said that the world was coming to an end in the year 1400. Naturally, in 1400, the Welsh peasants wanted to make the most of the time they had left; wine, women and fighting. They elected Owain Glyndŵr as their leader.

> *I promise to deliver my fellow countrymen from the oppression and the captivity they have suffered since the days of Cadwaladwr.*
> Owain Glyndŵr (1359–1415), Welsh ruler and the last native Welshman to hold the title Prince of Wales

That Welsh rebellion had shown a hatred for the English that extended to the females of the species.

Glyndŵr proclaimed:

> *I have been chosen, by God, to release the Welsh from the slavery of our English enemies.*

Owain Glyndŵr saw an opportunity to make a bid for independence while the English nation was unstable. In June 1402, Glyndŵr led his men on a raid into the border lands owned by the powerful Mortimer family. Villages were raided, and churches burnt. Mortimer was not a man to stand that sort of offence. He gathered his forces at Ludlow, recruited a good number of Welsh archers, and set off in pursuit.

But Owain's Welsh warriors only ran so far, then turned and faced their pursuers as the English marched along the Lugg Valley. Two thousand heavily armed Mortimer troops sweated uphill on a hot June day to chase a tactically withdrawn Welsh army half that size.

But the numbers were evened up when Mortimer's Welsh archers defected to join their mates in Glyndŵr's army. The result? A Welsh massacre of Mortimer's English.

So far, so chivalrous … well, maybe not the bit where the Welsh switched horses in mid-stream. But then came the revolting aftermath.

### Savage scavengers

> *We were in recycling before recycling was cool.*
>
> Anthony Pratt (b. 1961), Executive
> Chairman of Pratt Industries

Of course, the first recyclers were around thousands of years before the R-word word was coined. They were the battlefield scavengers. The peasants who wandered onto the battlefield, stripped the corpses of the fighters (both sides) and recycled weapons, clothing, loose change and spare food.

But after the battle of the Lugg they went a little further. You have to remember the Welsh had suffered a couple of years of depredations by Henry IV's troops. The Welsh peasants had suffered, and witnessed, many acts of brutality and rape. Now it was payback time and the women of the region were keen to get stuck in to the scavenging business … not just for the profits but from motives of revenge.

Chroniclers wrote of barbarous acts. Especially the female Welsh camp-followers who allegedly cut off the genitals of the dead English soldiers and stuffed them in the dead men's mouths. There were reports of them cutting off their noses and shoving them up their anuses. Nearly as bad (in the eyes of the devout writers), they denied the dead men a Christian burial.

As ever we have to look at the chroniclers themselves. Were they English scribes, inventing atrocities to portray the Welsh as savages? It's fairly certain the English dead lay unburied, and the stench pervaded the valley for months.

There was no Geneva Convention to say cutting off military meat-and-two-veg was a 'crime' per se. And, search as I might, I can't find the Geneva Convention specifically banning the cutting off of noses and inserting them where the sun don't shine.

But you wouldn't like it happening to you ... even if you were too dead at the time to know it was happening. War Crime? Or just a Welsh womanly joke in which the English dead were the butt of Welsh humour?

### *Lingering Lugg loathing*

The folk memory of this great Welsh victory lived on for centuries. The idea of British monarchs naming their oldest sons Prince of Wales caused resentment for centuries.

In 1911, the (Scottish-born) Rhondda MP Keir Hardie said at the investiture of a twentieth-century Prince of Wales:

> *There is to be a ceremony to remind us that an English king and his robber barons strove for ages to destroy the Welsh people. They succeeded in robbing them of their lands and driving them to the mountains like hunted beasts. The ceremony ought to make every Welshman blush with shame.*[10]

> Keir Hardie (1856–1915), Scottish socialist,
> politician and trade unionist

---

10. The British still have a non-Welsh Prince of Wales. Keir Hardie's words fell on deaf ears and those Welsh nationalists are still blushing red as a dragon's breath.

Chapter 3

# Wild Women

*For the female of the species is more deadly than the male.*
Rudyard Kipling (1865–1936),
English poet and novelist

A 2018 survey concluded that 80 per cent of modern crimes are committed by men. But when women turn to crime they don't mess about, as history demonstrates.

## Blackmail

*If you demand money from someone in exchange for your silence, it's called 'blackmail'. If your lawyer demands money from someone in exchange for your silence, it's called a 'settlement'.*
Arthur Baer (1886–1969), American journalist

### Ruthless reivers

The English-Scottish Borders were bleak places in mediaeval times. The peasants were hardy – or dead. They lived by farming sheep or cattle, but they also had the option of joining a gang, jumping on a pony and stealing from other Border farms. The thieves became known as 'reivers' and usually (but not always) these raids were carried out across the Border.

This suited the execrable Henry VIII very well, as the Borders in anarchic turmoil disrupted Scottish invasion plans. Henry was free to fry bigger fish ... like France.[1]

The reivers on both sides saw loyalty to royalty as a fluid thing. At the battle of Ancrum Moor (1545), Borderers switched sides in mid-battle, to ensure they ended fighting for victors. Pragmatic peasants. At the Battle of Pinkie Cleugh (1547), the Scottish and English Borderers were seen chatting to each other. When they realised they'd been spotted chewing the fat with their neighbour-enemies they put on a show of fighting.

Now, if you were a helpless farmer having your sheep and sleep ruined you could be offered an alternative. You were used to paying your landlord 'white male' (silver for rent). To the reivers you may choose to pay an unofficial rent to be left in peace – 'black male'.

The word became blackmail and adopted a more inclusive meaning: a demand involving threats to reveal true or false information about a person to the public, to a family member or the authorities.

The word may have been mediaeval, but the idea was as old as the Cheviot Hills. The Vikings had told English kings, 'Give our Danes a pot of gold and we'll leave you in peace.'

*And that is called paying the Dane-geld;*
*But we've proved it again and again,*
*That if once you have paid him the Dane-geld*
*You never get rid of the Dane.*

Rudyard Kipling

---

1. Had Mars Bars been invented he'd probably have fried those too.

## Murder in the Red Barn

*Squire William Corder: 'Didn't I make you a promise, Maria?*
*I promised to make you a bride. Don't be afraid, Maria. You*
*shall be a bride ... a bride of Death.' (Laughs maniacally)*

Randall Faye (1892 – 1948), American screenwriter, from the
movie *Maria Marten, or The Murder in the Red Barn*, 1935

The true tale of Maria Marten was the perfect peasant melodrama.

In 1828, in the little English village of Polstead, Suffolk, Mrs Marten said she was having a bad dream. The ghostly figure of her stepdaughter, Maria, appeared to her, pointing to a spot inside the nearby Red Barn – a local landmark.

She woke her husband and ordered him to go to the Red Barn and dig near one of the grain storage bins. He gathered his shovel and mole-spike and, with a few cronies, made his way to the Red Barn.

He poked the mole-spike into the hard earth of the barn floor but at one spot it sank deep into something soft. It came out with the spike covered in gore. Buried in a sack they found the rotting remains of his daughter, Maria. They knew her from her hair and clothing.

The coroner said that she had been murdered and ordered the arrest of the local squire, William Corder, the man Maria was supposed to have eloped to London with.

William Corder had been known as Foxy at school because of his sly ways; as a youth he'd been found guilty of forgery and stealing. His status as the squire's son kept him out of the local lock-up and he had wisely decamped to London after the trial.

Corder returned to Polstead when his brother, Thomas, drowned while trying to cross a frozen pond.

A lesson for us all.

*In skating over thin ice our safety is in our speed.*
Ralph Waldo Emerson (1803–1882),
American philosopher and poet

Then Corder's father and three brothers all died within the following eighteen months, and Corder and his mother were left to run the estate. Corder was an ugly little man, but with an attractive pot of gold that made him an Adonis to some gold-digging lady.

Enter the lowly peasant, mole-catcher's daughter Maria Marten. She was no innocent … though, of course, she was portrayed as such in the dramatisations of her tragic life. The melodramas soft-pedalled on the fact that she was older than Corder and her previous *liaisons amoureuse* had already resulted in two children. The father of the first child had been Corder's own brother, but the baby had died. The father of the second refused to marry her but sent money every month to provide for the child.

The future for Maria was bleak: a single mother stuck at home with an old father and a wicked stepmother. She saw Corder as the light at the end of the tunnel. In fact, he proved to be an oncoming train.

*A man in love is like a clipped coupon – it's time to cash in.*
Mae West (1893–1980),
American actress and comedian

Corder enjoyed the love of Maria – well, 'lust' may be a more appropriate term – but to marry so far beneath himself would see him become a social pariah. Then Maria announced to Corder that she was pregnant. The baby was born, and no wedding ring was in sight.

The baby died but Corder was not off the hook. Maria resorted to a little blackmail. Maria said she'd report him to the constabulary for the crime of bastardy.

The Poor Law of 1576 aimed to punish a bastard child's mother and father, and so relieve the parish from the cost of supporting mother and child. It was ordered that bastards should be supported by their fathers.

Maria also hinted that Corder had a hand in the baby's death. 'Marry me, Foxy, or go to prison,' was the not-so-subtle message. She had him by the proverbial short hairs. Blackmail.

Corder promised to do the decent thing and marry her. It was a promise he certainly never intended to keep, but he told her they could elope together and escape the shame of their situation. The promise bought him time.

> *My name is William Corder, to you I do declare,*
> *I courted Maria Marten, most beautiful and fair.*
> *I promised I would marry her, upon a certain day,*
> *Instead of that I was resolved to take her life away.*
>
> Victorian ballad

He told Maria to meet him in the Red Barn at midnight, dressed as a young man. He *claimed* that this would help to evade the bastardy net that he'd heard was closing around HER. (All heart was wily Will, eh?)

### The mother-in-law from Hell

> *I upset the wife's mother last Guy Fawkes Night. I fell off the bonfire.*
>
> Les Dawson (1931–1993), English comedian

Enter, stage left, Mrs Ann Marten – mole-catcher's wife and stepmother to Maria. She was just a couple of years older than

Maria, had a fractious relationship with her, and may even have fancied Corder's wealth herself. (Old Mr Mole-catcher Marten wouldn't be around much longer, would he?) So Corder enjoyed the attention of TWO gold-diggers.

The poorest of peasants, Maria and stepmother, saw him in relative wealth and it exaggerated their own poverty.

> *Where Plenty smiles – alas! she smiles for few,*
> *And those who taste not, yet behold her store,*
> *Are as the slaves that dig the golden ore,*
> *The wealth around them makes them doubly poor.*
>
> George Crabbe (1754 – 1832),
> English poet, in 'The Village'

Mrs Marten met Corder on his way to the Red Barn tryst. He was carrying a pickaxe and a spade. A bit of a clue there as to his intentions, Mrs Marten?

> *I then went home and fetched my gun, my pickaxe and my spade,*
> *I went into the Red Barn, and there I dug her grave.*
> *With heart so light, she thought no harm, to meet me she did go;*
> *I murdered her all in the barn and laid her body low.*
>
> Victorian ballad

Corder met Maria in the Red Barn.[2] As well as bastardy she accused him of stealing money sent by her living child's father.

---

2. The Red Barn wasn't red. A lean-to on the side of the thatched, wooden barn was roofed with red tiles. Another story says it was so named because, in the light of certain sunsets, it appeared red. By the time souvenir hunters had finished with it – or entrepreneurs who sold its planks as toothpicks – then the notorious Red Barn was one dead barn. The Martens' cottage in Polstead is still part of the tourist industry, now being run as a B&B.

When she refused to drop her threat of 'marry me, or else' he shot her and buried her under the barn floor. He moved to London but wrote regular letters to Mrs Marten and enclosed £5 with each one. Significant.

After a year the letters (and the money) stopped coming. Mrs Marten must have been angry and frustrated. Corder had got away with murder. What could she do? She could hardly go to the police and say, 'On the day Maria was last seen, a year ago, I saw him heading to meet her armed with a pickaxe and spade.'

'So why has it taken you a year to report this, Mrs Marten?' the constabulary would ask.

She could hardly reply, 'Because he's been sending me money to keep quiet. Blackmail.'

How could she reveal the murder without incriminating herself? She came up with the fantastical tale of Maria's ghost revealing the crime in a dream. A daughter's visitation to her dear mother seeking justice? (Let's overlook the fact that Maria WASN'T Ann's daughter and that they never much liked one another.)

The body was discovered, Corder arrested and brought to Bury St Edmunds for trial. The charge sheet was long:

⇨ The corpse had a bullet wound ... had she died from that?
⇨ She also had a wound to her neck ... was it Mole-catcher Marten's mole-spud that made the wound in the corpse, or had Corder stabbed her?
⇨ Corder's green handkerchief was tight around her neck ... had she survived the shot but been strangled as he dragged her to the grave with the handkerchief?
⇨ Or had she survived all these and suffocated in the grave?

Just to be on the safe side, Corder was charged with a dozen permutations of these murder methods. Done up like a kipper, was Corder. His defence was that he'd been in the barn but said they had argued. He had then left her alone only to hear a pistol shot as he was walking away. 'It was suicide, swelp me.'

Futile. The press and the public had decided the 'guilty' verdict before the trial even started.

> *After the horrible deed was done, she lay weltering in her gore,*
> *Her bleeding, mangled body I buried beneath the Red Barn floor.*
> *So, you young men that do pass by, with pity look on me,*
> *For murdering Maria Marten, I'll be hanged upon the tree.*
> Victorian ballad

Ann Marten, Maria's stepmother, testified about her dreams, and it took the jury only thirty-five minutes to find him guilty.

While awaiting execution Corder confessed to the prison chaplain to accidentally shooting Maria in the eye as she was changing into the man's clothing – her elopement disguise.

On the scaffold, just before the hood went over his head, he confessed again:

> *I am guilty; my sentence is just; I deserve my fate; and, may God have mercy on my soul.*
> William Corder's last words

### The punishment

From 7,000 to 20,000 ghouls turned up to witness Corder's execution. They had a gratifying piece of entertainment. It was before the days of the 'humane' trapdoor drop that broke the convicted person's neck. Corder was left to swing and choke slowly for over five minutes.

His indignities were not over.

⇨ His corpse was dissected in front of an audience of students and electric wires were attached to his body to demonstrate the contraction of muscles using electrical currents.

⇨ Pieces of the rope used to hang Corder sold for a guinea per inch.

⇨ Part of Corder's scalp with a shrivelled ear still attached was displayed in a shop in London's Oxford Street.

⇨ A lock of Maria's hair sold for two guineas

⇨ His corpse was skinned and used to bind a printed copy of the Red Barn story – it was put on display at Moyse's Hall Museum in Bury St Edmunds – it's still there.

⇨ His death mask was put on display and that's at the museum too.

⇨ His bones were assembled and used as a teaching aid at the Royal College of Surgeons. A series of tripwires made the skeletal hand rise up and point to the donations box when a visitor approached its glass case. The remains of the skeleton were not cremated till 2004.

⇨ His skull was kept as a souvenir by a Dr John Kilner – a collector of Red Barn memorabilia. But he was dogged by disaster and Corder's skull was eventually given a Christian burial in an attempt to lift the supposed curse.

⇨ The story of Maria and William was told in best-selling books, sermons, songs, peep shows, puppet shows and stage versions many times. These versions always showed Maria as the innocent maiden and William as the villainous squire.

⇨ In 1935 it was made into a movie starring Tod Slaughter (aged 50 playing Corder, actually aged 22) seducing Sophie Stewart (aged 30 playing Maria, aged 25). Mrs Marten (aged around 30) was played by Clare Greet (age 61). Spot the dramatic licence?

⇨ In 1980 it was revived (again) for television.

There you have it. Being blackmailed is bad enough, but murdering your blackmailer can be much, much worse. Like many peasants, Maria saw a land-owning member of the gentry as a few rungs up the social game of snakes and ladders. He saw her as a snake that had to be scotched, and that was his motive for murder.

Ann Marten's motive for blackmail? 'Greed', for the money Corder paid for her silence, and (perhaps) 'Revenge', for the fact he didn't follow up a courtship of her.

## Serial killing

### *The poisoners*

> *Blood's not thicker than money.*
>
> Groucho Marx

The Victorian era of crime is often remembered as the age of the poisoner.[3] And women indulged as often as men in what has been called (but not by me or by the victims) 'The Golden Age' of poisoning.

### *Adelaide Bartlett (1855 – ?)*

Adelaide Bartlett's husband, Edwin, was a Victorian murder victim who died of chloroform poisoning. Ed's post-mortem showed a large amount of liquid chloroform in his stomach, but no trace in the mouth or throat.

---

3. Oh, all right, it's remembered as the age of Jack the Ripper above all other crimes, but he (or she) was a one-off.

Liquid chloroform is almost impossible to swallow as it causes vomiting. How did it get there? Adelaide was acquitted at the trial. A surgeon at St Bartholomew's Hospital remarked, dryly:

*Now that she has been acquitted for murder and cannot be tried again, she should tell us in the interest of science how she did it.*
Sir James Paget (1814–1899), English surgeon and pathologist

Adelaide did not accept his invitation.

### Madeleine Smith (1835–1928)

The beautiful 21-year-old Madeline Smith lived in Glasgow in 1897. Madeline's father pressured her to become engaged to a friend of his, and she therefore tried to get passionate love letters back from her lover, Emile L'Angelier.

Emile not only refused to hand them over but threatened to show them to her new fiancé. Faced with disgrace, Madeline did what any of us would have done: poisoned him with arsenic in a cup of cocoa. Emile drank it and died.

Madeline went to trial but, remember, she was beautiful. Like with the Newcastle witchcraft suspect, the male jury went soft with lust and the final verdict was 'Not Proven' (a verdict only possible in Scotland).

### Florence Maybrick (1862–1941)

Florence was no Nightingale and decided arsenic would be just the tonic for her husband, James. No, seriously. Maybrick, a hypochondriac, was a regular user of arsenic and patent medicines. In small doses it had restorative powers. But, as well as hypochondria, he also suffered from a need to sow his wild oats like Jethro Tull's seed drill. Jim fathered five children with one of his mistresses. You may want to speculate that this was not a happy marriage and be unsurprised if Florrie wanted out … without the tiresome need of a divorce.

In 1889, after a short illness, James Maybrick died. Husband Jim's brothers were suspicious, and they searched the house like Maybrick Miss Marples. They found a packet labelled 'Arsenic. Poison for rats'. And, surprise, surprise, Maybrick's corpse revealed traces of arsenic in his stomach. Florence was sentenced to death, commuted to life imprisonment. She served fifteen years and was released in 1904.

### Mary Ann Cotton (1832–1873)

> *Mary Ann Cotton She's dead and she's rotten*
> *She lies on her bed with her eyes wide open*
> *Sing, sing, what shall I sing?*
> *Mary Ann Cotton is tied up with string*
> *Where? Where? Up in the air.*
> *Selling black puddings, a penny a pair.* [4]
>
> > Skipping rhyme of northern children
> > about Mary Ann Cotton's hanging

Adelaide, Madeleine and Florence. Probable poisoners who lived to tell the tale. But not Mary Ann Cotton. The others were middle class whilst Mary Ann was a peasant. She was a serial killer with an impressive record – impressive because she got away with it for so long.

---

4. The hanged corpse accumulates blood in the lower limbs, which swell and blacken. They end up looking like black puddings … but are not recommended for gourmet dining.

Her last victim was her downfall. Mary Ann was a coal miner's daughter but with dreams and aspirations above her neighbours. In 1872 she finally met the man who would make her dreams come true. His name was John Quick-Manning and he was a customs officer in the little Durham village of West Auckland. He was her escape hatch from a life of extreme poverty.

*There are people in whole parts of our cities who are being totally left behind and disregarded. They are unheard. And that extreme poverty breeds conditions for extreme violence.*
Martin O'Malley (b. 1961), American politician

Mary Ann lured the customs officer into her bed and, as was her custom, she became pregnant. Result. She had him lined up in the sights of her elephant gun. There was just one small problem. Little Charles Edward was son of Frederick Cotton, her (dead and poisoned) husband. He was her stepson – sort of – and was living with her.[5] As well as Fred Cotton, Charles Edward had witnessed the death of his baby half-brother, his aunt, and Mary Ann's lover. All by poisoning. How had he survived so long? Because Mary Ann had nothing to gain by his death … yet.

### Slips of the tongue

Mr John Quick-Manning didn't want Mary Ann to come with baggage. Charles Edward had to go. And still the boy had one last chance of survival: Mary Ann took the boy to the local parish officer, Thomas Riley, and asked him to put Charles Ed in the local workhouse.

---

5. If you want to be picky, Charles Edward was the son of Fred Cotton whom she married … but bigamously. So, was he strictly speaking her stepson? Take out a mortgage and pay a lawyer to answer that one.

Riley's reply was the seal on Charles Edward's fate: the boy could only go in the workhouse if Mary Ann accompanied him. Mary Ann hadn't murdered her way to her top prize to end up in a workhouse. In that moment Charles Edward's fate was signed and sealing waxed. And, a moment later, the furious Mary Ann slipped the noose round her own neck, for she replied spitefully:

*Never mind, I won't be troubled long. He'll go like all the rest of the Cottons.*

Parish Officer Riley was startled. The little boy looked perfectly well – weedy and undernourished, but not sickly. He was astonished when, just a week later, Charles Ed was dead and the indifferent doctor diagnosed 'gastric fever' … like the rest of the Cottons. Riley went to the constable with his suspicions.

The doctor tested the stomach contents of the dead child and found they contained arsenic. A lot of arsenic. Mary Ann could have escaped but delayed her departure till she could claim the dead child's insurance – as she had for most of her victims. But without a death certificate there would be no payout.

That delay allowed the local newspaper to investigate her past and discovered she had been unlucky in love – three dead husbands and a lover – and perhaps eleven of her thirteen children.

At her trial she was badly defended because – unlike middle-class Adelaide, Madeleine and Florence – she couldn't afford a half-decent defence lawyer.

To murder so many she must have had a psychopathic condition. Children were clearly a burden and their murder could be seen as retrospective terminations. She swore her innocence, but the law was relentless.

John Quick-Manning's intervention may have helped her, but he vanished from the scene. She was sentenced to hang. While she carried Quick-Manning's child she could not be hanged. But after its birth in Durham gaol she took the short trip and the long drop of the gallows. Only that drop wasn't long enough.

### Slow death

William Calcraft was the executioner. Mary Ann Cotton died, not from her neck breaking, but by strangulation caused by the rope being too short, possibly deliberately. Calcraft used the short-drop hanging method in which the victim was slowly strangled to death over several minutes. To hasten death Calcraft would sometimes theatrically pull on legs or climb on shoulders to break a condemned criminal's neck. Some say Calcraft used this method to entertain the crowds, who numbered 30,000 or more.

The moral of the story? If you want to poison your husband, then be middle class and you could well get away with it. If you're a peasant? Try divorce.

## Infanticide

*A woman concerned in baby farming at Warsaw has been charged with murdering seventy-five infants. She was sentenced to 3 years' imprisonment.*

*Bathurst Free Press and Mining Journal*, Australia, 1890

The Industrial Revolution often meant misery to the masses. There hadn't been a lot of joy in their lives *before* the machines of mass production arrived.

It was legal in the Georgian era to capture vagrant children and force them into apprenticeships: slavery in all but name. Some were shackled to prevent them escaping, with irons riveted on their ankles, and they were forced to walk, work and sleep that way.

At first the younger children could prove useful additions to the workforce … their skinny bodies could wriggle under the machines. But the humanitarian classes persuaded the government to pass child protection laws. The first prohibited children under ten from working underground. Two years later, another Act was passed prohibiting the textile industry from employing children younger than nine.

But …

*Nothing happens in a vacuum in life: every action has a series of consequences, and sometimes it takes a long time to fully understand the consequences of our actions.*
Khaled Hosseini (b. 1965), Afghan-born<br>American novelist and doctor

The upper classes had nurseries and nannies (or public schools). Before the days of au pairs even the middle classes farmed out their children to peasants in the village.[6] But the peasants themselves didn't always have that option.

If children (and especially babies) couldn't be taken to work, then what did you do? Stay at home, lose your wage-earning capacity and starve? Or go to work and pay someone else to look after your child?

The single woman was vulnerable to exploitation by both men and other women. If she fell pregnant, and the father abrogated responsibility, she was in a bad place ...

---

6. Jane Austen was fostered in this manner, as were all her siblings, from a few months old until they were toddlers. Did she go willingly? Or was there some Persuasion involved?

⇨ Pregnancy out of wedlock was a mortal sin.
⇨ Many families ostracised their 'fallen' daughter.
⇨ She could travel to another city where she could give birth anonymously.
⇨ Abortion was illegal.
⇨ Infant mortality rate was high and unwanted children would be a financial burden.
⇨ With luck she'd be allowed back into the family fold if she returned without the baby.

But one person's problem is another's opportunity. And that's where the service of the 'baby farmer' emerged. The baby farmer was paid to look after unwanted children.[7]

> Poor girls who fell down from the straight path of virtue,
> What could they do with a child in their arms?
> The fault they committed they could not undo,
> So, the baby was sent to the cruel baby farm.
>
> Victorian street ballad

### Amelia Elizabeth Dyer (1837–1896)

> Toleration is the greatest gift of the mind; it requires the same effort of the brain that it takes to balance oneself on a bicycle.
> Helen Keller (1880–1968), American author and political activist

Very well, Ms Keller. Before we tear into the evils of baby faming let's be tolerant and give the other side of the story.

Many baby farmers had no evil intent; in fact, some of the baby farmers were good-hearted women. They went on caring

---

7. 'Baby farmer' was a pejorative term for someone paid to take your child off your hands. Today we prefer to call them 'school teachers'.

for their little darlings even when the birth mother could no longer pay. These carers were sometimes childless women who did just what their adverts proclaimed – they adopted a child and treated it as if it were their own.

Is that balanced enough? Because, sadly, some baby farmers were as evil as any human on earth. Baby farmers like Amelia Dyer.

In April 1896, Reading police had discovered the bodies of two infants in the river Thames. They had been strangled with white tape, wrapped in parcel paper and dumped in a carpet bag.

It was the third dead baby that led them to the 'motherly' midwife who lived in a two-up-two-down, rented terraced house on Kensington Road in London. What they discovered shocked them.

Now the amazing thing was how she got away with it for so long. Harold Shipman (1946–2004) escaped detection of his 250+ victims because he was a doctor.

Amelia Dyer killed 400 or more – in over twenty years – even though she was too careless to be left in charge of a boiled egg. She was so careless she wrapped the infant corpses in brown wrapping paper that had the name of one of her aliases and address written on it.[8]

Her home was crammed with damning evidence:

⇨ dozens of vaccination papers
⇨ large quantities of children's clothing
⇨ numerous pawn tickets for baby clothes
⇨ letters and receipts for newspaper advertisements
⇨ ... and the heavy stench of rotting flesh coming from the kitchen pantry and from a trunk under her bed.

---

8. She may have been a mass murderer, but at least she helped save the planet with her recycling efforts.

The police ordered the dragging of the river adjacent to the baby farm and found parcels of dead babies, each weighted down with a brick. The Reading body count rose to fifty, and Amelia told the police:

*You'll know all mine by the tape around their necks.*

Investigative journalists discovered she'd been trading in infanticide for almost thirty years, from Liverpool to Plymouth.

She began work in Bristol in the late 1860s and charged a fee to take in unmarried women when they could no longer hide their pregnancies. Dyer's early crimes were murder-to-order, as some of her clients asked for their infants to be stifled at the moment of birth. It was their little secret as forensic science couldn't distinguish between stillbirth and suffocation.

The ones who survived the birth – but were abandoned by their mothers for a fee – were slowly starved. Liberal doses of an opiate (laudanum) or cheap gin quieted both the baby's appetite and its cries.

So much suffering could have been avoided if there had been better regulation of Victorian childcare. For, after ten years of her murderous career, Dyer had been apprehended for infant neglect and served a six-month sentence. Yet she was released to resume her grim trade.

She switched to full adoption for a one-off payment. No more laudanum or slow demises. The children lasted just hours. Dyer used a length of white tape wrapped twice around their necks. She slipped the little corpses into the nearest rivers or buried them in the gardens of her lodgings.

The mounting mortality rate was never a national media scandal; reports of infant bodies on the streets of the underclasses were too common to be considered newsworthy.

Dyer's total can only be guessed at … and guesses range from a minimum of 300 to over 400. She wasn't the only murderous British baby farmer, but she was certainly the most prolific.

She became a household name, as ballad-mongers wrote songs about her; her case raised the profile of the fledgling NSPCC and even firmed up Britain's adoption and child protection laws. Yet within a few decades, her criminal career was all but forgotten.

The white ribbons, and the wrapping-paper shrouds that had her name on, suggest the interesting psychological possibility that she 'wanted' to be caught. Otherwise we have to assume she got careless or was quite stupid.

Her defence lawyers tried to prove insanity – she had been twice committed to asylums in Bristol – but failed to convince the jury, who took just five minutes to find her guilty. They must have decided the heinous scale of her crime didn't warrant any merciful mitigation. She was sentenced to hang.

*On account of her weight and the softness of the textures, rather a short drop was given. It proved to be quite sufficient.*
Prison Commission file logs Dyer's final
moments at Newgate Gaol, 1896

She became known as 'The Ogress of Reading'.[9] Her ghost was said to haunt Newgate Prison.

---

9. 'Ogress of Reading' is not a pretty epitaph, but in 1939 a writer tried to prove she was also a candidate for the title 'Jack the Ripper' … along with over a hundred other names including Lewis Carroll. Not so much a red herring as a white rabbit. If you want to sell books, then accuse someone new of being Jack. Me? I have incontrovertible evidence it was Queen Victoria.

## Scottish savagery

> *It seems rather hard to run down a woman,*
> *But this one was hardly a woman at all,*
> *To make a fine living in ways so inhuman,*
> *Carousing in comfort on poor girls' downfall.*
>
> Victorian street ballad

In 1888, a group of boys played football with a paper parcel. When the paper split it revealed a dead baby inside, aged about a year. The baby's father had given the baby to Jessie King to look after. He paid the woman £5.

Baby farmers took the parents' money and promised to look after the child. If the child died quickly then the baby farmer made a good profit. If the baby DIDN'T die 'naturally' then the baby farmer sometimes 'helped' it to die.

Jessie King gave the baby whisky to keep it quiet and she said the whisky killed the child by accident. But the doctor said it was strangled.

Jessie King was hanged – the last woman to be hanged in Edinburgh. She was the ultimate capitalist.

> *Capitalism is the worst friend of humanity.*
> Evo Morales (b. 1959), 80th President of Bolivia

Some baby farmers may well have seen themselves as performing a service to the unmarried mothers whose babies they suffocated at birth.

It was easy money for someone whose conscience had long since been anaesthetised. People like Amelia Dyer clearly suffered from 'criminal, or amoral behaviour without empathy or remorse'. Around the time of Amelia Dyer a new word was coined that fitted that psychological profile: 'psychopath'.

# Chapter 4

# Tudor Twisters

*The cony-catchers, apparelled like honest civil gentlemen or good fellows, with a smooth face, as if butter would not melt in their mouths.*

Robert Greene (1558 – 1592), English dramatist, poet, pamphleteer, rake and debauchee

## Swindling

Confidence tricksters have been preying on human stupidity, human weakness and human greed since the serpent conned Adam into nibbling a Pink Lady.

Tudor London was a dangerous place. If a prigger didn't steal your prancer (horse) or a courbers didn't drag your goods out through the window with a long hooked pole, then a foist would pick your pocket or a nip may cut off that purse that you dangled so conveniently, temptingly and stupidly from your belt.

We know the wily ways of the worldly-wise city swindlers because of Robert Greene's pamphlets. And Green was not just an observer or a vigilante; he was a shrewd operator himself. He eloped with a wealthy woman, spent her money, then abandoned her (and child) for the sister of a notorious character of the London underworld.[1] (Greene's lover was described as 'a sorry ragged quean', or a Greene quean if you prefer.)

---

1. The criminal was known as 'Cutting Ball' and he ended his life hanged at Tyburn. With a name like Cutting Ball it makes one's eyes water to think of how he acquired his notoriety.

He disappeared into the stews of London among the whores, thieves and lowlifes. He made a living from writing plays (six), poetry and pamphlets ... mostly love stories – a sort of early romantic novelist. Mills and Greene perhaps?

Greene was probably the son of a Norwich saddler and, like so many of his background through history, they were:

*touched with a burning ambition.*
*To shake off their lowly born tags, yes they try.*
Peter Sarstedt (1941 – 2017), British singer and lyricist

Greene is remembered for making the first reference to Will Shakespeare's work. Shakespeare had written of a:

*tiger's heart wrapped in a women's hide.*
*Henry VI*

But Greene saw Will as a bumpkin, not worthy to grace the London stage. How dare this playwright-poet, Stratford son-of-a-glovemaker upstart try to outshine the university-taught gentlemen? Greene spat:

*For there is an upstart Crow, beautified with our feathers, that with his Tigers heart wrapped in a Players hide, supposes he is as well able to bombast out a blank verse as the best of you: and being an absolute Johannes factotum, is in his own conceit the only Shake-scene in a country.*
Robert Greene, *Groats-Worth of Wit*

That's rich coming from the playwright-poet, Norwich son-of-a-saddler upstart.

But Greene's bitter and jealous diatribe aside, he is a useful source of low-class crime in the city. He wrote a warning to visitors and wrote as a reformed villain. A Trip Advisor to low-life crime.

### Cony-catchers (swindlers)

First assemble your team of confidence tricksters, each with a role …

> *THERE be requisite effectually to act the art of cony-catching three several parties: the Setter, the Verser, and the Barnacle. The nature of the Setter, is to draw any person to drink with him, which person they call the Cony.*

Then the game's afoot.

> *As soon as they see a plain country fellow then, 'There is a cony,' saith one. At that word out flies the Setter, and overtaking the man, begins to salute him thus:*
> *'Sir, God save you, you are welcome to London, how doth all our good friends in the country, I hope they be all in health? Why sir,' saith the Setter, 'I know you by your face & have been in your company before, I pray let me crave your name and the place of your abode.'*
> *The simple man straight tells him where he dwells, his name, and who be his next neighbours.*

Even the dullest peasant will deny he knows the Setter, and that is the opening the cony-catcher has been waiting for. He slaps his forehead and begs forgiveness …

> *Yet hold me excused, for I took you for a friend of mine, but since by mistaking I have made you slack your business, we'll drink a quart of wine, or a pot of ale together.*

If the cony accepts then he is lured into the tavern. If he refuses, then the Setter passes on the victim's name and info to the 'Verser'. The Verser then manages to meet the victim in the street and greets him, by name, as an old friend. He uses all the information the Setter gained.

> *'Have you forgot me? why I am X's kinsman, your neighbour not far off: we'll drink afore we part.'*

Once in the tavern the cony is invited to play a crooked game of cards. The Verser identifies the 'Barnacle' – the third member of the gang. The Verser whispers to the cony that the Barnacle is a rich, but dim, gentleman. Between them they can win a nice pot of silver. But after a winning streak, it is the Barnacle who scoops the pot and the cony who is relieved of all his money.

Another lure is to have the Verser accost the cony and – again using the Setter's information – claim he has friends in the cony's county. Will the cony deliver a letter for the Verser? Well, the letter's not written yet but if he'd care to enter the tavern for a little while, then ... you get the picture.

### Mumchance no-chance

> *Gambling: The sure way of getting nothing for something.*
> Wilson Mizner (1876–1933), American playwright,
> raconteur and entrepreneur

The most popular game for the Verser and Barnacle was a simple one – no need for the cony to worry about the rules. It looks like a game of luck. It is called Mumchance at Cards.

You need a pack of playing cards and two or more players. To play:

⇨ The cards are shuffled and placed face down on a table.
⇨ Each player in turn calls the name of a card – everyone has to name a different card.
⇨ The cards are turned over one at a time.
⇨ The player whose card is turned over first wins a point.
⇨ First to ten points is the winner.

Advanced play: Do not shuffle the cards each time but place the turned cards to one side. Good players will remember which cards have been turned over and will not name them.

But if you are looking for a guide to making a fortune from pub-mugs, that still leaves the game to chance. The cony-catchers of Tudor Britain practised sleight of hand so they knew the way the cards would fall.

### The ticket scam

Other tricks included selling tickets for plays – at a cut price, naturally. But those plays were never performed. A man called Richard Vennor tried this and pocketed all the money. But, in the end, he was caught and thrown in prison.

At first Vennor used his ill-gotten money to buy a private cell in the gaol. He could afford good food and wine from the gaoler. But, when the money ran out, he was thrown in 'The Hole' with fifty other men, women and children to sleep on bare boards. The cold in winter or the disease in summer or the bad food killed anyone who stayed too long.

> *In the hole you are buried before you are dead.*
> Thomas Dekker (1572–1632), Elizabethan dramatist

Richard Vennor died.

And in Bury St Edmunds, a shoemaker was tricked by a card cozener. A few months later, he happened to see the man arrested and taken to court for another offence. When the cozener pleaded he was a gentleman the shoemaker spoke up and exposed him as a card sharp. The cozener was sentenced to a whipping. As the shoemaker had no chance of recovering his money he asked if he could administer the whipping and the judge agreed.

*He made him pay an ounce of blood for every pound of silver.*

Robert Greene

Cozening can be bad for your health.

### Cross-biting

Greene described cross-biting cons as men who extort money from a prostitute's clients by pretending to be her husband. Just as he is about to enjoy the 'pleasures' of the prostitute, her husband bursts in and demands the victim's purse or he will be thrashed or disgraced in the law courts.

That's a familiar trick to this day, of course, and certainly far older than Elizabethan times.

As Greene wrote:

*I mean a dishonourable art, when a base rogue, either keepeth a whore as his friend, or marries one to be his maintainer, and with her not only cross-bites men of good calling, but especially poor ignorant country farmers, who God wot be by them led like sheep to the slaughter.*

The naïve country peasant is the victim of the town peasant.

Greene leaves all of us with a warning about cozening and cross-biting:

*Thus, gentle readers, have I given you a light in brief, what I mean to prosecute at large and to all Justices, that they will seek to root out these roguish arts.*
*I commit you to the Almighty.*

It was Greene who was soon committed to the Almighty. He died at the age of 34. According to a rival pamphleteer, Gabriel Harvey, Greene died from:

*a surfeit of pickle herring and Rhenish wine.*

## Conspiracy to murder

*If you're going to do something wrong, do it big, because the punishment is the same either way.*
                    Jayne Mansfield (1932–1967), American actress

Harsh punishments don't appear to have deterred criminals. And none were harsher than in torturous Tudor times.

In King's Lynn, Norfolk, Margaret Day was a poor servant. In 1531 she poisoned the family she worked for. A man would have been hanged; Margaret was sentenced to be boiled alive. She was lowered into boiling water time and again till she died. As she died it is said her heart exploded from her chest and hit the wall of a house opposite.

*Stone walls do not a prison make, nor iron bars a cage.*
                    Richard Lovelace (1617–1657), English poet

But, Richard, stone walls DO keep bursting hearts out of your breakfast cornflakes.

## Hubby trouble

*A good wife always forgives her husband when she's wrong.*
Milton Berle (1908 – 2002),
American comedian and actor

Many of the underclasses committed murder because they aspired to be upwardly mobile. Alice Arden was an exception. Alice Arden (1516 – 1551) was a well-born woman who conspired to have her husband, Thomas Arden, brutally murdered so she could be with her low-born lover, Richard Moseby.

Alice Brigantine married Thomas Arden and made their home at Faversham Abbey. They had at least one daughter, Margaret, born in 1538.

She began an affair with Moseby and carried on fairly openly. Hubby, Thomas, must have known but, like Nelson, turned a blind eye. Alice's family were well connected and her usefulness outweighed her infidelity, Thomas calculated. But ignoring Alice's bit of rough on the side was a mistake. A fatal mistake.

Alice's ardour for Arden had cooled like Mummy Bear's porridge. And speaking of porridge, she laced Tom's with poison. It was a fairly pungent poison and the man ate a couple of spoonfuls before complaining it tasted unpleasant. He must have suspected, yet still he stayed married to awful Alice.

What she needed was a team. It would end up as a five-a-side team ... on Alice's side.

First recruit was John Green, a Faversham tailor who had lost a land dispute with Alice's husband and already come to blows with him. Thomas Arden's servant was recruited to help. For good measure they drew in George Bradshaw, a Faversham goldsmith and ex-soldier. Now they needed a professional killer. And Bradshaw had a friend who was making a living as a highwayman, hitman and thug. Black Will of Calais – what an impressive name. He was the man for the job and ten pounds was his fee.

He was well worth the money. A real enthusiast. When John Green pointed out the target, Will was straining at the leash.

> *Green, at the time appointed, showed Black Will Mr Arden walking in St Paul's upon which Black Will asked him: 'Who is he that follows him?'*
>
> *'Marry,' said Green, 'one of his men.'*
>
> *'By my blood,' quoth Will, 'I'll kill them both.'*
>
> *'Nay,' said Green, 'do not do that, for he is in the secret.'*
>
> *'By my blood, I care not for that, I will kill them both,' replied he.*
>
> *'By no means,' said Green. Then Black Will proposed to murder Mr Arden in Paul's Churchyard, but there were so many gentlemen with him that he could not affect it.*
>
> From *The Newgate Calendar*, a monthly bulletin of executions, produced by the Keeper of Newgate Prison in London

If at first you don't succeed, fail, fail and fail again.

Several attempts of Black Will failed – firstly the servant (in on the plot) locked the doors to Arden's London house when he was supposed to leave them open for Will. He feared (with good reason) for his own life. By my blood but that got Will's blood up.

Then, on their ride home to Faversham, they reached Rochester and the servant made an excuse to leave Arden to ride on alone – and open to Will's wiles. But Arden met a bunch of friends on the road and was by my blood saved again.

Black Will recruited an equally odious mate with an equally interesting name: George Shakebag. Arden was due to ride to a ferry to the Isle of Sheppey. Will and Shakebag were primed to intercept him. This time Black Will managed to get himself lost. Where's your sat-nav saddle when you need one?

## Valentine's Day massacre

*Today is Valentine's Day – or, as men like to call it, Extortion Day.*

Jay Leno (b. 1950), American comedian, actor and TV host

On his way home from Sheppey, Arden took a different route and the killers missed him again. It was close to Valentine's Day. The plotters decided that would be an apt day to finish the job. This time Black Will would hide in a cupboard in the Arden parlour and ... bop.

Low-class lover Mosby was squeamish but adorable Alice persuaded him to join the Valentine's Day party. Mosby played cards with the victim while servant Michael stood behind Arden's chair. Black Will leapt out and strangled Arden while Mosby smashed the man over the head with a clothes iron.

Black Will made certain with a slash to the head with his sword; he was paid and rode away, (by my blood), on Green's horse. But Alice wasn't satisfied. She took a knife and stabbed the corpse seven or eight times. The cool lady mopped up then invited a couple of guests to supper.

*Then Mosbie's sister was sent for, and sat down with them, and they were all very merry.*

*Newgate Calendar*

If you can't be merry after disposing of an unwanted husband then when can you be, eh, Alice?

*When supper was over, Mrs Arden made her daughter play on the virginals, and they danced, and she amongst them.*

*Newgate Calendar*

The guests were Alice's alibi. When they were gone, the men dumped the body in a snowy field. Alice told the townsfolk Thomas had gone missing and wept 'the tears of a crocodile' (as *Newgate Calendar* expressed it).

### Snow show

As plotters go, the Alice Arden team weren't too bright. The mayor arranged a posse to search for Tom and, when he was found, the searchers noticed lots of footprints in the snow leading to the Arden house. Alice in Blunderland.

Alice was questioned and denied that she would ever harm her beloved husband. But, when confronted with the knife she'd used, her resistance cracked and she groaned:

> *Oh, the blood of God help me, for this blood have I shed.*
>
> *Newgate Calendar*

Her loyalty to her murder team was somewhere between nil and zero as she betrayed them all. The men were duly hanged, but Alice (and one other maid) were women. They hadn't killed an 'equal', they had killed a man ... a superior being. And, as a citizen killing a king, that was a form of treason – petty treason. The punishment was burning.

Curiously, Black Will died by burning too, for an unrelated crime.

> *Will escaped for many years, but was at length taken, and burnt on a scaffold at Flushing.*
>
> Raphael Holinshed (1529–1580), English chronicler

### *The play's the thing*

The murder story was an Elizabethan sensation and the play *Arden of Faversham* has continued to entertain audiences to this day. Was the black comedy written by William Shakespeare? Some experts think so. As the Alice character frantically attempts to clean up, she says:

> *Alice Arden: The blood cleavest to the ground and will not out.*

Words that echo another play about bloody murder.

> *Lady Macbeth: 'Out, damned spot. Out, I say. ... Yet who would have thought the old man to have had so much blood in him?*
>
> *Macbeth*, Act V Scene i

So, Alice and her maid suffered the grim punishment of being burned at the stake. All because they were women.
As a world-famous philosopher said:

> *Women who seek to be equal with men lack ambition.*
> Marilyn Monroe (1926–1962), American actress

### Vagrancy

> *A honest man is seldom a vagrant.*
> Cato the Younger (95 BC–46 BC),
> Roman statesman and stoic philosopher

When the Black Death struck Britain in 1349, a law was passed making 'idleness' a criminal offence. The lords lost half their peasant labourer force to the plague, so compelling any vagrant to work would help ease the manpower crisis.

The targets of the law were not the impotent poor, who were too frail or sick to work, but the healthy idlers. In 1530, Henry VIII (a healthy idler par excellence) had a law passed:

*Beggars who are old and incapable of working must receive a beggar's licence. But there must be whipping and imprisonment for sturdy vagabonds.*

The law was quite detailed about the punishment:

*They are to be tied to the cart-tail and whipped until the blood streams from their bodies.*

The old feudal idea remained: a person 'belongs' to his place of origin and it is that town/parish's responsibility.

*They are to swear on oath to go back to their birthplace or to serve where they have lived the last three years and to put themselves to labour.*

That philosophy has been replaced by the idea that the unemployed should go out and seek work ...

*I grew up in the 30s with an unemployed father. He didn't riot; he got on his bike and looked for work and he kept looking 'til he found it.*

Norman Tebbit (b. 1931), speech to the
Conservative Party Conference, 1981

Mr Tebbit's father would have been stopped by PC Plod in Henry VIII's day and sent back to his home (where there was no work). So, it's good to see we have progressed over those 400 years: we now have bikes.

Mr Tebbit stopped short of recommending a return to the birch for the wilfully unemployed. Henry VIII was less blushingly coy:

> *For the second arrest for vagabondage the whipping is to be repeated and half the ear sliced off.*

That would damage a wandering minstrel's chances of finding a job. Let's face it; you need to have a good ear for music.

Would you, sturdy vagabond, care to wander off again?

> *For the third relapse the offender is to be executed as a hardened criminal and enemy of the common weal.*

You don't do a lot of tramping the countryside with a noose around your neck. Then, in 1547, Henry's son, Edward VI, came up with a new twist to the tramp problem.[2] The vigilante system. If you see a vagrant, then report them to the magistrates or constables and get a really practical reward. The 1547 Act said:

> *If anyone refuses to work, he shall be condemned as a slave to the person who has denounced him as an idler. The master has the right to force him to do any work, no matter how vile, with whip and chains.*

An offer too good to refuse. Report an idler and they become your slave for two years and YOU can become … well, an idler. And that slave can't run away without harsh consequences.

---

2. In fairness, little Edward probably just squiggled his name on the act. The initiative came from his uncle, Edward Seymour, who took the role of Lord Protector.

*If the slave is absent for a fortnight, he is condemned to slavery for life and is to be branded on forehead or back with the letter S; if he runs away three times, he is to be executed as a felon.*

*If it happens that a vagabond has been idling about for three days, he is to be taken to his birthplace, branded with a red-hot iron with the letter V on his breast, and set to work, in chains, on the roads or at some other labour.*

*Every master may put an iron ring round the neck, arms or legs of his slave, by which to know him more easily.*

The enslaved vagabonds were to be fed bread and water or a small drink and were allowed to be worked by beating, chaining, or other methods the master may choose.

If you didn't especially want that vagabond slave, then you could sell him/her. And if no one wanted that slave they had to return to the parish where they were born and do community service, repairing roads.

A vagabond child could be claimed as an 'apprentice' and be kept working for a minimum wage till he was 24 (20 for a girl). Given the short lifespan of a Tudor person, that's practically a life sentence. Should they attempt to escape this apprenticeship, they were treated as a slave.

The problem was, the laws were so harsh that the local authorities were reluctant to enforce them and that 1547 Act was repealed after just three years.

*To make a thief, make an owner; to create a crime, create laws.*

Ursula K. Le Guin (1929 – 2018), American novelist

But vagrancy remained a crime throughout the century and beggars were regularly whipped and imprisoned in 'Houses of Correction'.

Vagrancy is often linked to begging.

## Begging

*My loving people*
*I know I have the body of a weak, feeble woman; but I have*
*the heart and stomach of a king, and of a king of England*
*too. I myself will take up arms, I myself will be your general,*
*judge, and rewarder of every one of your virtues in the field.*
Queen Elizabeth I, speech at Tilbury after the Armada victory

There's a lot of debate as to whether Elizabeth ever made this speech, first reported twenty years after her death. But it seems unlikely that she would really 'take up arms' and fight side by side with her people. Other reports said she ran away to hide when the Armada was sighted.

One soldier was punished for saying that, when the Armada arrived:

*she was 'pissing herself with fear'.*

And if she *had* taken up arms it would have been in vain. By the time she rode to Tilbury she knew full well that the Armada was wrecked and posed no danger. The queen refused to return, for her own safety, to London, declaring that:

*I would not think of deserting my army at a time of danger.*

She probably felt safer surrounded by 8,000 armed men.

### Thank you and goodnight

But those men cost money, and that hurt Elizabeth. The cost of her forces in Kent and Essex (the likely invasion areas) came to £783 14s 8d per day. The moment she was assured of her safety the queen ordered an immediate demobilisation of the army.

An interesting (and unremembered) sentence from that famous speech:

*I know already, for your forwardness you have deserved rewards and crowns; and We do assure you on a word of a prince, they shall be duly paid.*

So, it's, 'Thanks guys. You done good. Time to reward you like Premier League footballers.'

And that is one of the most hollow promises in the history of the Hollow Crown. The soldiers were sent home, and many joined the unemployed. But the sailors suffered worse.

The commander of the English Fleet, Lord Effingham (1536–1624) wrote to the queen's councillors to say:

*Sickness and mortality begins wonderfully to grow amongst us; and it is a most pitiful sight to see, how the men, having no place to receive them into here, die in the streets. I am driven myself, of force, to come a-land, to see them bestowed in some lodging; and the best I can get is barns and such outhouses; and the relief is small that I can provide for them here. It would grieve any man's heart to see them that have served so valiantly to die so miserably.*

Many were given only enough money for their journey home, with some receiving only part of the pay due to them. Lord Howard of Effingham paid many sailors from his own purse, saying:

*I would rather have never a penny in the world, than they should lack*

As for Elizabeth, who had assured them (on a word of a prince), they should be duly paid? She washed her hands of her fighting men and drove them to begging. Her officers then used the laws against begging to punish them.

Elizabeth's treasury passed the wage bill to the ports. The ports claimed poverty and tried to pass it back to the Crown. Meanwhile the men survived by begging ... or starved.

And finally, the government found a solution for the men who survived to get back to their home parishes. The sailors were *given a licence to beg*. For a limited period.

William Browne lost an arm in the Armada fighting and was permitted to beg 'in all churches' for a period of a year.

Those veteran sailors and soldiers who dared to complain were subject to punishment. Elizabeth's government ordered:

*The queen does straightly command sailors and soldiers to forebear to make disordered assemblies, upon pain of imprisonment.*

Adding insult to injury, she insisted on taking every penny of her share of the treasures looted from the Spanish galleons.

### Queen of clubs

A year later, Elizabeth's indifference turned to active persecution when she ordered:

*the apprehension and punishment of soldiers, mariners and other vagrant and masterless persons and sturdy vagabonds.*

Borrowing her dad's 'sturdy vagabonds' term, she actively sought to stop them from begging with the raging rant that complained:

*These ragged rabblements of rakehells that, under the pretence of great misery, do win great alms.*

And constables like Edward Langridge of East Grinstead were themselves punished if they failed to enforce her Draconian rules. Langridge's crime?

*Allowing some rogues or idle wandering people to walk and wander up and down.*

Finally, five years after the Armada had vanished, people like Robert Mackey received compensation to relieve them of the need to beg. Mackey had lost his hands in a battle and received 33 shillings and 4 pence. Enough to last him all of two months … a month for each hand.

And Elizabeth? A pamphlet told of how the mere sight of beggars upset her:

*The Queen is troubled, whenever she takes the air, with these miserable creatures.*

Shame. Elizabeth I's treasury was bare, and she had to soldier on with a mere 3,000 gowns and 628 pieces of jewellery.

**Plus ça change …** *spare a bit of change?*

And in the days of Elizabeth II, a councillor in Windsor argued:

*There is a growing concern amongst residents, businesses and visitors regarding the number of people occupying the streets of Windsor, who are begging during the day and in some cases taking the occupancy throughout the night.*

He demanded police use legal powers to clear the area of homeless people before a royal wedding – Elizabeth II's grandson – in May 2018. (Echoes of 'The Queen is troubled, whenever she takes the air,' perhaps?)

Elizabeth I or Elizabeth II, the peasant underclasses are still the target of the ruling upper classes. An exception made the headlines when a judge regretted the situation.

*I will be sending a man to prison for asking for food when he was hungry.*

British judge jailing a man for four months for begging,
*The Guardian*, 20 May 2018

In a separate case, a man was fined £105 after a child dropped £2 in his sleeping bag. The ragged rabblements of rakehells do still win great alms then.

Chapter 5

# Sinful Stuarts

*Tremble, thou wretch,*
*That has within thee undivulged crimes*
*Unwhipped of justice.*

William Shakespeare (1564–1616),

*King Lear*

The Stuart era saw the end of the Tudors then the end of Will Shakespeare. Scots took over the kingdom. King Charlie was chopped, and Oliver Cromwell's Puritans created crimes where none existed before. Celebrating Christmas would be punished. Witches were hanged in England and burned in Scotland.

Punishments were still harsh. Around the year 1700, Mary Channing was just 14 when her parents forced her to marry Richard Channing. By the time she was 19 she'd had enough, so she poisoned him.

She was taken to the old stone circle known as Maumbury Rings near Dorchester. Over 10,000 people gathered to watch her being strangled. Then they cheered as her body was burned.

In 1767, people were still being taken to that ancient circle to be executed in public.

## Robbery with violence

*Pity is treason.*

Maximilien Robespierre (1758–1794),
French politician, and leading figure
in the French Reign of Terror

### William Spiggot (1691–1721)

Robbery with violence must be one of the oldest crimes in history. Taking candy from a baby is easier than taking the baby from a Rottweiler so of course the bullies of this world will try stealing candy if they think they can avoid the consequences.

William Spiggot was a bully. He was accused of highway robbery and violent theft, and faced execution. He came up with a plan to avoid the scaffold. He would simply refuse to plead either guilty or not guilty ... so the trial could not proceed.

A cracking idea but soon the only thing cracking would be his ribs. For the law had anticipated this eventuality and said that a criminal who refused to plead would be subject to *Peine forte et dure* – literally, 'hard and forceful punishment'. He would be pressed with weights until he pleaded – or died.

A witness in the 1400s described what would happen to the prisoner:

> *He will lie upon his back, with his head covered and his feet, and one arm will be drawn to one quarter of the house with a cord, and the other arm to another quarter, and in the same manner it will be done with his legs; and let there be laid upon his body iron and stone, as much as he can bear, or more.*

92

Spiggot's partner in crime gibbered like a babbling brook as soon as he understood what would happen. Spiggot remained silent and took the weights with groans of 'Pray for me'.

He also complained about a heavy weight on his head, according the *Newgate Calendar*. There were no weights on his head but the blood was being forced from his body into his face and it felt that way.

After half an hour, 50 pounds (about 23 kg) had been added on his chest and that was as much as he could take. He agreed to return to court and plead not guilty. He was hanged anyway. The bully had been bullied to defeat.

> *The greatest evil is physical pain.*
>> Saint Augustine (354 – 430), Christian
>> theologian and philosopher from Numidia

William Spiggot had been outlasted by a woman, Margaret Clitherow of York, who had refused to plead and bore the same pain to the death.

### Remember, remember Margaret

> *Let us all be brave enough to die the death of a martyr, but let no one lust for martyrdom.*
>> Mahatma Gandhi (1869 – 1948), Indian leader

To deny that Elizabeth I was the head of the Church in England (as Roman Catholics of the age did) was treason, for which the penalty was death by hanging. Margaret hid Catholic priests from Tudor persecution and was caught.

At trial she knew that a guilty plea would see her assets confiscated by the state and her children left destitute. If she pleaded not guilty then her children would be interrogated –

under torture if necessary – to betray her. She couldn't win, so she remained silent.

Margaret was stripped and had a handkerchief tied across her face. A sharp rock was placed under her back in the hope it would break her spine and give a mercifully quick release.

The door from her own house was put on top of her – symbolic. But the sergeants ordered to carry out the execution hadn't the stomach for it. They hired some desperate beggars instead. They loaded the door with rocks and stones weighing at least 700 pounds (320 kg). Death came within fifteen minutes, but her body was left for six hours before the weight was removed. She was pregnant with her fourth child.

The queen (a week or so too late) wrote to the people of York to say Margaret Clitheroe should not have been executed. Of course, rather than weaken the Catholic cause, this martyr strengthened it.

*Did you know ...*

Margaret Clitheroe was executed in York in March 1586. At that time the city was the home of a 6-year-old Protestant boy. If the boy didn't witness Margaret's crushing then he must have heard the grim details in his school – because schoolboys are like that – or in his family. The boy went on to convert to Catholicism and planned to fight back against the oppressors of the Catholics. Was he inspired by the injustice to Margaret?

The boy's name was Guy Fawkes.

*Pressing engagements*

Torture brings out the worst in human nature. John Weekes (died 1731), accused of highway robbery and murder, refused to plead. He was tortured and pressed in public, in the marketplace in Horsham. He was laid on his back and stone weights were piled on top of him in increments, until Weekes lay under 400 pounds of boulders. So far, so conventional. But then the report says:

*He was [almost] dead, having all the agonies of death upon him. Then the executioner, who weighs 16 or 17 stone, lay down upon the board which was over him, and adding to the weight, killed him in an instant.*

A merciful end to his suffering? Or, as other reports suggest, a bit of sport for the spectators as the executioner used Weekes as a bouncy castle?

### Sarah Malcolm (1711–1733)

*Sarah Malcolm was given a good education at school in Reading, Writing and such other Things as are proper for a Girl, above the meanest Rank of People.*

*Newgate Calendar*

Sarah wasn't born into peasanthood – she was above 'the meanest of people'. Her father was a respectable Durham man with an estate worth £100 a year. Sadly, he had extravagant tastes and dragged the family into poverty.

*Too many people spend money they earned, to buy things they don't want, to impress people that they don't like.*
Will Rogers (1879–1935), American cowboy and humourist

Sarah found work in a 'low' public house, The Black Horse, then she became laundress to a number of residents who lodged in chambers above the London Inns of Court. Sarah fell into 'bad company' – always a good excuse when you are caught doing wrong. She met Mrs Mary Tracey, and her friends, the young brothers James and Thomas Alexander. They encouraged her to cheat and steal from her employers. 'You have access to their homes when you do their laundry, Sarah. Take advantage,' they must have said.[1]

When she discovered her 80-year-old neighbour, Widow Lydia Duncomb, had a nest egg she would stop at nothing to lay her hands on it. She certainly didn't stop at the widow's housemates: 60-year-old Betty (her companion) and Anne (17), their maid.

One February morning in 1733, Anne was found with her throat cut from ear to ear. Betty and Widow Duncomb had been strangled. Sarah was blamed.

Savage Sarah's apron was found under her bed and was covered with blood; her bloody dress was found stuffed down the toilet. A silver tankard with blood on the handle was found in Sarah's room – she claimed it was a gift from her mother. A hoard of gold coins were found hidden in her hair, and her explanation was that she'd found them in the street. Sarah's hair would have been thick and greasy and tied up on her head, but to use it as a purse is straining credulity. Sarah told the jailer who found the money to keep it – he reported her attempted bribery.

Sarah didn't simply dream of climbing from the meanest of people. She had real drive.

> *Ambition is a dream with a V8 engine.*
> Elvis Presley (1935 – 1977),
> American singer

---

1. They forgot to mention Sarah would be a prime suspect and the trio of tempters weren't putting their own heads in Tyburn nooses. They were arrested but later walked free.

It didn't need Sherlock Holmes to solve the triple murder or even modern forensic science. Our question would be, 'How on earth did she expect to get away with it?'

And the answer is that she blamed Tracey and the Alexanders. She said she was just the lookout and that she knew nothing about the murders. So how did you get blood all over your clothes, Ms Malcolm, eh? She shocked the all-male jury by telling them it was menstrual blood, and it probably detracted from her defence.

In any event, the robbery itself was a capital offence – simply admitting being part of a gang of thieves was a death sentence.[2] She cross-examined every witness herself in minute detail. That turned a simple case into a five-hour trial. The jury made up for the tedious hours by taking just fifteen minutes to deliberate and come up with a 'guilty' verdict.

Crimes committed by a young woman were rare, so she had her moment of fame. A celebrity. The well-known painter William Hogarth visited her in prison a couple of days before her execution and drew her portrait. He sketched her before they stretched her.

*When you become a celebrity, the world owns you and your image.*

Megan Fox (b. 1986), American actress and model

Sarah was sent to be hanged and looked very smart in a black dress and black gloves. Thousands of people turned out to see her so platforms were built to give the crowds a really good view. (And an attempt to cash in on human misery by some scaffolding entrepreneurs.) Pickpockets had a field day.

---

2. Two men had already hanged at Tyburn that year for robbery without murder.

Marino Branch
Brainse Marino
Tel: 83367

The rickety platforms collapsed, and dozens of people were hurt. Those who came to see a woman suffer were themselves left bruised and bleeding. It's hard not to feel a malicious pleasure at the irony of that.

*To feel envy is human, to savour schadenfreude is devilish.*
Arthur Schopenhauer (1788–1860),
German philosopher

She never really confessed to the murders – she left a document that was more a list of self-justification – but was distressed to find she'd be hanged at Fleet Street, where she'd worked and where her acquaintances and neighbours would witness it.

Sarah was stood on the back of a cart and a rope was put round her neck by her hangman – 'Laughing Jack' Hooper.

Jack (probably laughing) gave the horse a sharp slap on its flanks, causing the steed, and the cart, to move away and leave Sarah swinging and kicking for some considerable time in the empty air. She was 22 and there is a theory that she had fallen in love with one of the Alexander brothers and stole to free herself from servitude and marry. It's a plausible motive, but still the waste of her life and those of her victims.

Yet in a way, Sarah was LUCKY. If she had been Widow Duncomb's servant she would NOT have been hanged – the punishment for a servant killing her mistress was to be burned alive at the stake.

## Duelling

*Sometimes in politics one must duel with skunks, but no one should be fool enough to allow skunks to choose the weapons.*
Joseph Cannon (1836–1926),
American politician

Duelling is armed combat between two people, with matched weapons, invariably subject to 'rules'. People (usually men) have always attempted to batter one another. Cave men probably had clubs at dawn. But there developed a 'code' as chivalry evolved.

Posh people learned it at knight school. Posh people duelled, peasants had punch-ups. Yet, just occasionally in history, one of the underclasses sorted out his differences with a formal duel. The most striking duellist was probably Lord Minimus, who – despite his title – was peasant born and bred. He was also a person of restricted growth.

### Lord Minimus

Jeffrey Hudson was born to average sized parents in England's smallest county, Rutland, in 1619. Jeff was tiny, yet perfectly proportioned. His father, a son of the soil, tended the cattle of the 1st Duke of Buckingham, George Villers, and on his seventh birthday young Jeffrey Hudson was presented before the Duchess of Buckingham as a 'fine rarity of nature'.

The duchess was so tickled with the little man who stood only half a metre tall that she invited him to join the household. He didn't rise from peasant status to servant class. He sank to freak show exhibit.

*Clowns are the pegs on which the circus is hung.*
P.T. Barnum (1810–1891), American showman

The duke and duchess entertained King Charles and at the climax of the celebration, a pie was placed before the queen. Jeffrey burst through the crust, dressed in a tiny suit of armour to the surprise and delight of all.

The queen had a passion for collecting rarities and simply had to add Jeffrey to her collection. He was 'owned'.

His new housemates included a Welsh giant, William Evans, and two dwarves. In circus slang he was a midget; in medical terms he was a pituitary dwarf. Was he humiliated by being part of the queen's freak show? Or was he philosophical?

> *My advice to other disabled people would be, concentrate on things your disability doesn't prevent you doing well, and don't regret the things it interferes with. Don't be disabled in spirit as well as physically.*
> Stephen Hawking (1942 – 2018), English physicist

Jeffrey was taught the manners of the court as well as how to ride a horse and shoot a pistol. In 1642 he travelled with the queen to the Netherlands to raise money and support for King Charles, but returned to find the English Civil War was raging. Hudson was appointed a 'Captain of Horse' but as the war turned against Charles he had to flee with the queen to France.

By now Hudson took his rank quite seriously. He stood for no insults or jests at his expense. When insulted by the brother of William Crofts he challenged the man to a duel.

Hudson chose pistols on horseback and all that pistol training stood him in good stead. He shot Crofts through the head. But duelling was as illegal in France as it was in England. The dead man's brother, William Crofts, another of the Queen's Masters of Horse, was furious. He demanded that the queen bring Hudson to justice. Hudson's punishment was to be sent from her court.

His mistake was to shoot to kill. Noble duellists like the Duke of Wellington fought for principle, not for blood. In 1829, when he was Prime Minister, Wellington challenged an opponent, Lord Winchilsea, to a duel. Both men fired to miss. Winchilsea apologised, and Wellington went back to Downing Street, honour satisfied.

Jeffrey Hudson, Lord Minimus, duelled the peasant way with a bullet to the brain assuaging his anger (and assuaging the life of Crofts).

*Did you know ...*

Jeffrey was lucky he hadn't been fighting in the reign of Henry II (reigned 1154–1189). Thomas of Elderfield duelled with George of Northway and was defeated. The law demanded that Thomas's eyes be gouged out by George's family.[3]

Hudson's life spiralled downwards till he was thrown into prison in 1680 for his Catholic beliefs and died a few years later, a penniless pauper, back to where he started. The wheel of fate had turned a full circle.

## Witchcraft

*For all those witch-women, my sisters,*
*who breathed freer*
*as the flames took them,*

*knowing as they shed*
*their female bodies,*
*the seared flesh falling like fruit*
*in the flames,*

*that death alone would cleanse them*
*of the sin for which they died*

*the sin of being born a woman,*
*who is more than the sum*
*of her parts.*

Erica Jong (née Mann, b. 1942),
American novelist and poet

---

3. It is recorded that Thomas was nursed back to health by St Wulfstan in Worcester. His eyes were miraculously restored.

Witchcraft was an odd sort of crime because it only existed in the minds of some of the accusers and a few of the unfortunates who tried to practise their magic.

The idea that people could work in league with the Devil to pervert the natural laws was ancient. Laws against it were laid down in the Old Testament and the punishment was unequivocal:

> *Thou shalt not suffer a witch to live.*
>
> King James Bible, Exodus 22:18

And if that isn't explicit enough:

> *A man also or woman that hath a familiar spirit, or that is a wizard, shall surely be put to death: they shall stone them with stones: their blood shall be upon them.*
>
> King James Bible, Leviticus 20:27

Very fitting that the quotes are from the *King James* version of the Bible because it was that King James (I of Scotland and VI of England) who was obsessed with witchcraft himself.

He believed there were several black magic plots to kill him before he came to the English throne. He even wrote a book about witchcraft. One of his perverted pleasures was to watch witches being tortured.

Yet witchcraft was not made a capital offence in Britain until 1563 – forty years before James succeeded to the throne of England. It WAS seen as 'heresy' and was deemed such by Pope Innocent VIII in 1484. From 1484 until around 1750, some 200,000 witches were tortured, burnt or hanged in Western Europe.

Many unfortunate men and women were condemned on a phantasmagoria of evidence and hanged after undergoing appalling torture. The 'pilnie-winks' (thumb screws) and iron 'caspie-claws' (a form of leg irons heated over a brazier) usually got a confession from the unfortunates accused on James VI's watch.

### Hunt the witch

*Witchcraft is one of the most baseless, absurd, disgusting and silly of all the humbugs.*

P.T. Barnum

P.T. Barnum made part of his fortune by promoting famous hoaxes. He charged the public to see the remarkably small 'Tom Thumb', a diminutive 11-year-old. Well, he would look like a diminutive eleven years old since the lad was only four. A hoax.

Barnum was just one of a long and dishonourable line of people who perpetrated frauds on the public. As Barnum himself said:

*Nobody ever lost a dollar by underestimating the taste of the American public.*

He could have omitted 'American' and been just as accurate. But Barnum was harmless. Others were deadly, especially for the poor.

In the 1640s, a man called Matthew Hopkins (a failed lawyer) became the self-proclaimed 'Witchfinder General'. He had sixty-eight people put to death in Bury St Edmunds alone, and nineteen hanged at Chelmsford in a single day.

Hopkins' theories of deduction were based on The Devil's Marks. A wart or mole or even a fleabite he took to be a Devil's Mark and he used his 'jabbing needle' to see if these marks were insensitive to pain. His 'needle' was a 3-inch long spike, which retracted into the spring-loaded handle so the unfortunate woman never felt any pain.

There were other ways of testing a witch. Mary Sutton of Bedford had her thumbs tied to opposite big toes and she was thrown into the river. If she floated she was guilty, if she sank, innocent. The unfortunate Mary floated. Hopkins was responsible for over 300 executions.

Urban myth said he was condemned and hanged as a witch himself in a neat irony. Sadly, that is certainly untrue.

Witchcraft in Britain was mainly a peasant practice. From Saxon times, villages had their 'cunning folk' who offered healing with natural remedies and the odd spells or incantations, conjurations and charms.

The peasants were not fools and in their own minds were quite clear about harmful witchcraft – with the help of the Devil. The cunning folk were a medical service who predated the NHS by half a millennium. (And in another half-millennium, the NHS may catch up.)

It wasn't the 'criminal' witches who created the crime. It was *the law*. And, as we all know:

'If the law supposes that,' said Mr Bumble, squeezing his hat emphatically in both hands, 'the law is a ass – a idiot.'

Charles Dickens, *Oliver Twist*, 1838

And the law was an ass when the asinine King Henry VIII allowed a law to be passed in the Witchcraft Act of 1542. It targeted both witches and cunning folk without distinguishing them. The penalty was death.

This law was repealed around five years later when sensible Edward VI was briefly on the throne. But in 1563, big sis Elizabeth I saw a bill was passed by Parliament designed to illegalise 'Conjurations, Enchantments and Witchcrafts' – again failing to distinguish between witches and the cunning folk.

The punishments were not so harsh and may have lain forgotten in the vaults of forgotten legislation. But the witch hunt that had been raging in Scotland and in much of Europe finally arrived in England.

And where there is fear there is someone waiting to cash in on it. Throw in some anger you have against some neighbour and you have a double-edged weapon. Fear and anger drove the witch hunts.

*Con men look for human frailty to exploit. This is most often greed. Trump found a different vice: anger. The emotional are always the most susceptible to manipulation.*

Pamela Meyer, American author
and certified fraud examiner

### Town Moor terror

*Bill of charges for the witches for 2 weeks ending 23th of August 1650 and other charges for executing the prisoners.*
*£15 19s 2d.*

Accounts of the Newcastle Chamberlain

Newcastle witch trials saw thirty suspects tried in the town hall, and fifteen were executed on the Town Moor. So, it seems, you CAN put a price on a life. Just over ten bob in old money back in 1650.

The world-famous half-marathon race, the Great North Run, starts alongside the Newcastle Town Moor. The 50,000 runners may feel they are about to face a torturous hour or three. They mostly don't realise that they line up alongside what was once the most horrible place in the city. Because this is the place where criminals were executed in public – the guilty as well as the innocent.

All the Newcastle so-called witches were women, except for one man who was found to be a wizard who, it was said, could turn himself into a black cat.

Witch hunts had spread panic among the British populace and Newcastle Council didn't want to be left behind in the righteous rally to root out these devil-worshippers. The Puritan Town Corporation were thrilled. The councillors didn't know how to spot a witch themselves. However, along came a 'successful' Scottish conman. A local MP said this savage Scot:

*professeth himself an artist in that way.*

This artist – or con-artist if you prefer – had had thirty alleged witches executed on the Border at Berwick, then found his way to Newcastle by December 1649. All he had to do was see if there were any witches in Newcastle.

For each successful prosecution he'd receive a pound. The average daily wage at that time was less than three pence.

Pay a man richly for results and you will get results, by hook or by crook. And the witch-finder was certainly a crook. But he found some unexpected (or maybe not-so-unexpected) cronies … the good folk of Newcastle Town.

The Newcastle town crier walked through the town asking for:

*all people that would bring in any complaint against any woman for a witch.*

Do YOU have a grudge against a neighbour? What an opportunity to stick the knife in … or rather, the bodkin. For the test of the accused involved partially stripping the women and pricking them with a bodkin on a Devil's Mark.

If they bled, they were innocent. If not, they were guilty.

Amid the horrors of our human ancestors there are many forgotten heroes who should remind us that in the midst of darkness there is a light of kindness. Ralph Gardiner wrote a book in which he looked at the brutal public humiliations visited on citizens of the town and took testimonies relating to the witch trials. You have to respect the bravery of his witnesses in standing up to the witch-finder. One woman whom Gardiner spoke to – Elinor Loumsdale – had actually been prosecuted for trying to dissuade witnesses giving evidence against the accused.

The most controversial accused was a quite handsome and well-presented young woman. Gardiner described how the woman had been 'pricked' by the witch-finder and had not bled so of course she should be hanged. But ...

*A 41-inch bust and a lot of perseverance will get you more than a cup of coffee – a lot more.*

Jayne Mansfield

Lieutenant Colonel Hobson had witnessed the spectacle. The witch-finder had pulled up the woman's clothes and exposed her, much to her embarrassment. He then appeared to prick her thigh just as he let her skirts fall about her. This obscured the actual 'pricking'.

The woman confessed she felt nothing – so she was condemned by her own words. Hobson (a Baptist not a Puritan), an ex-military surgeon, suspected a trick on the part of the witch-finder. The allure of the woman may have spurred him like a white knight to her defence.

*The reputed Witch-finder acquainted Lieutenant Colonel Hobson that he knew women, whether they were Witches or no simply by their looks.*

*The Colonel replied and said, 'Surely this woman is none, and need not be tried.'*
*The witch-finder's reply was that, 'The Town said she was, and therefore he would try her.'*
Ralph Gardiner's *England's grievance discovered*, 1655

A pretty face – or a 41-inch bust – carried no weight with the witch-finder, but in this case, Hobson insisted that the pricking be repeated (in a more decent manner). This time the woman bled and was acquitted.

Nevertheless, the remaining accused seventeen women and one man were hanged on the Town Moor in August 1650. Their remains were buried in unmarked graves in St Andrew's Church, Newcastle.

*These poor souls never confessed anything, but pleaded innocence.*
*One, by the name of Margaret Brown, had beseeched God that some remarkable sign might be seen at the time of her execution.*
*And as soon as she was turned off the ladder her blood gushed upon the people to the admiration of the beholders.*
Ralph Gardiner's England's grievance discovered, 1655

*Aftermath*

You'll be pleased to hear the witch-finder was suspected of fraud and arrested in Scotland. He admitted sending 220 innocent people to their deaths. And he was hanged. A sort of justice. But no consolation for the innocent victims or their families.

Until the middle of the 1800s, Newcastle's Town Moor was used for public executions – the east gate from the city was known as the Gallows-gate and Newcastle Football ground still has its Gallowgate End.

The English gave up hanging witches during the reign of James II – the last unlucky woman was Alice Mulholland – and they didn't have any more witch trials after 1712.

The Scots went on persecuting witches a little longer. The last to be burned for witchcraft in Scotland was in 1722.

Women were still 'ducked' on a stool into freezing water if they nagged too much. That nasty habit went on until 1817, when Sarah Leeke was ducked. It all ended as a bit of a joke – when Sarah Leeke was ducked they couldn't get her under the water. The pool they'd chosen was too shallow.

### The last witch

*After seeing a smiling 'medium' at a psychic fair, a friend of mine punched her. When I asked him why he would do such a thing, he replied, 'My father always taught me to strike a happy medium.'*

In 1944, Helen Duncan was a Scottish spiritual medium, working in Portsmouth. She began broadcasting information from the port's gullible sailors who came to consult her. D-Day was approaching and she was a security risk. She had to be stopped.

Duncan was originally charged under the Vagrancy Act 1824, relating to fortune telling, astrology and spiritualism. Then there was a change of plan. The paranoid government's legal experts sent her to be tried by jury at the Old Bailey for contravening section 4 of the Witchcraft Act 1735, which carried the heavier penalty of a prison sentence.

Winston Churchill even described the whole episode as 'obsolete tomfoolery' but Helen went to prison for nine months.

The 1753 Act was later repealed and replaced with the Fraudulent Mediums Act of 1951.

So, no more witch trials.

You could call it hex-it.

Marino Branch
Brainse Marino
Tel: 8336?9?

## Animal cruelty

*Brutality to an animal is cruelty to mankind – it is only the difference in the victim.*
Alphonse de Lamartine (1790–1869), French poet

While the lords hunted their deer and wild boars the peasants enjoyed equally murderous 'sports', setting cocks to fight or dogs to tear each other apart.

Not that lords were indifferent to watching animal cruelty. Henry VIII had a bear pit built at Whitehall and Elizabeth I was also fond of the sport. As she processed around the south her hosts provided it as entertainment. Brutal? No ...

*It was a very pleasant sport, of these beasts, to see the bear with his pink eyes leering after his enemies approach.*
D.J. Ribton-Turner, *Vagrants and Vagrancy and Beggars and Begging*, 1887

The Tudors and Stuarts were able to enjoy fine literature and depravity of cruelty to animals side by side. Shakespeare's plays were performed to groundlings and lords alike in the same theatres. And even a noble mind like Shakespeare could cash in on the popularity of the bear-baiting in the theatre by introducing one of the animals into the performance.

*Exit, pursued by a bear.*
Shakespeare's stage directions – leading
up to the offstage death of Antigonus, *The Winter's Tale*[4]

---

4. There's some speculation that this could have been an actor dressed in a bear costume.

The Tudors saw the rise of the Puritans (bless them) and an opposition to this form of entertainment. Because of the suffering of the animals? No. Because people were daring to have fun on a Sunday. God, it seems, was happy to witness his creatures butcher one another on any other day of the week.

It seems foreign visitors were a little puzzled, but not too disgusted, by a British obsession with this pastime.

*June 23, 1710: Towards evening we drove to see the bull-baiting, which is held here nearly every Monday in two places. On the morning of the day the bull, or any other creature that is to be baited, is led round. It takes place in a large open space or courtyard, on two sides of which high benches have been made for the spectators. First – a young ox or bull was led in and fastened by a long rope to an iron ring in the middle of the yard; then about thirty dogs, two or three at a time, were let loose on him but he made short work of them, goring them and tossing them high in the air above the height of the first storey. Then amid shouts and yells the butchers to whom the dogs belonged sprang forward and caught their beasts right side up to break their fall. They had to keep hold of the dogs to hinder them from returning to the attack without barking. Several had such a grip of the bull's throat or ear that their mouths had to be forced open with poles. When the bull had stood it tolerably long, they brought out a small bear and tied him up in the same fashion. As soon as the dogs had at him, he stood up on his hind legs and gave some terrific buffets; but if one of them got at his skin he rolled about in such a fashion that the dogs thought themselves lucky if they came out safe from beneath him. But the most diverting, and worst of all, was a common little ass, who was brought out saddled with an ape on his back. As soon as a couple of dogs had been let loose on him, he broke into a prodigious gallop – for he was free, not having been tied up like the other beasts – and he stamped and bit all round himself. The ape began to scream most terribly for fear of falling off. If the dogs came too near him, he seized them with his mouth and twirled them round, shaking them so much that they howled prodigiously. Finally another bull appeared, on whom several crackers had been hung: when these were lit and several dogs let loose on him on a sudden, there was a monstrous hurly-burly. And thus was concluded this truly English sport, which vastly delights this nation but to me seemed nothing very special.*

Zacharius von Uffenbach (1683 – 1734),

German scholar and traveller

In 1760, bull-baiting was finally banned in Newcastle upon Tyne. A young sailor who was spectating was gored in an accident – he must have been gutted. The 'sport' was banned because it was dangerous to the public, *not* because it was cruel to the animals.

It wasn't until 1835 that baiting was banned by Parliament by the Cruelty to Animals Act. Passing a law is one thing, enforcing it another.

*Dogs forced into fighting suffer terrible injuries, both from the fights and at the hands of their vicious 'owners'. Most will ultimately be killed in the ring or die soon after from their injuries. Those who can no longer fight are often brutally dispatched.*

League Against Cruel Sports report, 2018

Cockfighting thrives too …

**Cockfighting where roosters battle to the death at FIVE-YEAR high in UK, figures warn**

*New figures reveal that the number of incidents of the cruel blood sport has shot up by a quarter.*

Daily Express, 15 August 2017

## Vigilante justice

*The more corrupt the state, the more numerous the laws.*

Tacitus (c. 56 – c. 120), Roman senator and historian

For hundreds of years the state was allowed to kill its citizens. But were the citizens allowed to kill one another? Oh, no they weren't. Call that justice? This anomaly infuriated some people who came up with the obvious answer – do-it-yourself retribution.

These people are often known as vigilantes … because vigilantes sounds more glamorous than lawless, anarchic thugs. They are invariably bullies because they set out to exact their revenge in the certain knowledge their victims are not in a position to resist them. (The notable exception being David v. Goliath, but even David had the advantage of a guided missile.)

These self-righteous seekers after justness are probably inspired by fictional vigilantes, from the Lone Ranger to Batman, the Avengers to Charlie's Angels, but real vigilantism from history tells tales that are usually tawdry.

*Actual Bodily Harm*

### The Knobstick avenger

*I've got a friend who is a lion tamer. He used to be a school teacher till he lost his nerve.*

Les Dawson (1931–1993),
English comedian, actor and writer

In the 1890s, Sarah-Anne Knobstick was caned by her teacher, Miss Dorothy Trimmer, in Lirriper Lane Board School in London.

Screaming Sarah ran home to tell mum, Katherine Knobstick, who was furious with indignation. 'How dare a teacher beat my child – that's my job.'

She set out to avenge the injustice. She marched straight to the school, burst through the door and grabbed Miss Trimmer.

First she assaulted the teacher verbally, using language more suited to a seaman. Her threats were imaginative and graphic:

*I am going to throw a kettle of boiling water over you, then I am going to rip out your heart with my bare hands and use your heartstrings as laces in my corsets.*

Katherine Knobstick

The purple-faced parent grabbed the teacher by the hair, tearing out lumps. A punch sent the terrified trainer to the floor, the perfect place for Mrs Knobstick to give her a taste of her toecaps.

The maternal mauler was taken to court and fined the considerable sum of 40 shillings (around £200 today). Was Mrs K repentant? She was not. Her defiant statement after the trial was:

*It was worth every penny.*

*Fraudulently procuring a marriage*

### The Knobstick wedding

*Definition of knobstick:*
*A stick, can, or club with a rounded knob at its head.*

While we are on the subject of knobsticks, let's look at the dubious peasant practice of the knobstick wedding. The upper classes may call it a shotgun wedding but if you can't afford a shotgun then a big stick will persuade a man to marry a woman he has impregnated outside of marriage.

Or, in the 1829 case of the unfortunate William Saxton, a woman he DIDN'T have the pleasure of impregnating.

The vigilantes in this 1829 case were in fact Parish Officers Philip Bateman and David Walker, whose day job was supervising the workhouse at Middleton in Derbyshire.

Their peasant victim was William Saxton, described as a 'slender-witted man, twenty-four years of age'.

The buxom bride was Lydia Brooks, some fifteen years older, who had a wooden leg. Both of the happy couple were paupers. Bateman and Walker decided that their workhouse charges should tie the knot of respectability in church and bribed and threatened slender-witted Saxton into marrying his peg-legged and pregnant princess.

William Saxton's bewildered defence sounds convincing:

*I never know'd Liddie Brooks, but she sweared a child on me as soon as she'd gotten to Middleton. So when she'd swear'd it, they sent o'er for me to filiate it. Because I kno'd nothing about it, they remanded me to Wirksworth gaol. When I had lied in gaol some time, the gentlemen I telled you of comes to me, and says they: 'Why, man, you mun marry this lass.'*

*'Ay,' says I: 'I mun as well, sin you mak me father o' her bairns.' Then says they again: 'If you don't you know you'll lie in gaol for a twelvemonth, and happen be hanged after all. ... They gied me some liquor, and I being scared, gied 'em my promise.'*

Handcuffed, hatless, shoeless and inebriated, the pauper was taken from goal to Matlock, where a licence of marriage was obtained and paid for by the overseers. In the morning the overseers took him to church, where his wooden-legged bride awaited him.

Saxton took her for better or for worse – and almost certainly for poorer or for poorer. He was convinced that the choice was a hangman's rope or being joined in holy deadlock.

Eventually – but too late to save Saxton – the overseers were summoned before a magistrate for their part in the Knobstick wedding. What happened to the men who had fraudulently procured a marriage?

Nothing, of course. They were acquitted.[5]

And Saxton's life sentence married to the limping lady of the workhouse? He left her after two days of married bliss.[6]

*A man inserted an 'ad' in the newspaper: 'Wife wanted.'*
*Next day he received a hundred letters. They all said the same thing: 'You can have mine.'*

Anonymous

---

5. I hope you do not suspect the judges of colluding with the parish officers to find their mates not guilty? After all, they were law-abiding citizens whilst falsely imprisoned Saxton was a mere peasant. That is like suggesting a police officer could be corrupt. Shame on you.
6. Did he tell her to hop it?

# Chapter 6

# Quaint Crimes

*I can take any empty space and call it a bare stage. A man walks across this empty space, whilst someone else is watching him, and this is all that is needed for an act of theatre to be engaged.*

Peter Brook (b. 1925), English theatre and film director

Crime is news. The human race, to which so many of my readers belong, is fascinated by the misdeeds of others. A crime is only a crime when it is uncovered. If no one knows of the crime then it isn't a crime, is it?[1] We need the criminal *and* the shocked voyeur – you.

Humans *want* to know about crime and that's what keeps news sources in business. But the more unusual an event, the more interested readers are. We are all so filled with curiosity.

*The first and simplest emotion which we discover in the human mind, is curiosity.*

Edmund Burke (1730–1797), Irish statesman, author and
philosopher

---

1. For example, the phrase 'The human race, to which so many of my readers belong' was stolen by me from G.K. Chesterton (1874–1936) without his permission. I'm a plagiarist. A thiever of words. But if I hadn't confessed, no one might have known and no crime would have been committed. Now I *have* confessed I will complete this manuscript from a prison cell, I suppose.

And the curiouser[2] the crime, the more curious the reader. As journalists say, 'You never read about a plane that did not crash.' And, as *New York Sun* editor said:

> *When a dog bites a man, that is not news, because it happens so often. But if a man bites a dog, that is news.*
>
> John B. Bogart (1848–1921)

## Quackery

> *The trouble with being a hypochondriac these days is that antibiotics have cured all the good diseases.*

Where there is human misery there will be someone, somewhere who will find a way to exploit it. There have been few greater miseries than the Black Death, which arrived in Britain in 1348.

It wiped out swathes of the population and was explained as a punishment from God. A priest used the wrath of God as an opportunity to attack children and the high mortality rate amongst the young. He said:

> *It may be that children suffer heaven's revenge because they miss going to church or because they despise their fathers and mothers. God kills children with the plague – as you can see every day – because, according to the old law, children who are rebels (or disobedient to their parents) are punished by death.*[3]

---

2. Blame Lewis Carroll for that quaintly cobbled word. 'Curiouser and curiouser,' cried Alice (she was so much surprised, that for the moment she quite forgot how to speak good English).
3. The Scots believed God was punishing the evil English. They invaded the north of England, where their soldiers caught the plague and took it home. Hard to feel sorry for them as the plague spread through Scotland. An own goal that scored a kick in the Trossachs.

To avoid the disease, the rich were able to flee to the countryside, where the lower population density helped to decrease its spread. The peasants were tied to their villages and suffered, helpless.

Most historians guesstimate that the Black Death killed half the population. In some places like the village of West Thickley in County Durham, it killed everyone. The death rate was high in monasteries, where the monks prayed together, stayed together and cared for one other. Till death do they part.

## Crazy cures

The word 'quack' comes from the old Dutch word quacksalver – someone who quacks (boasts) about the virtue of his salves or medicines. And they thrived in the days of the plague, playing on the terror of the people.

The Black Death exaggerated the divide between rich and poor. The peasants made do with simple cures based on superstition rather than sense. They …

⇨ killed all the cats and dogs in the town
⇨ ate cooked onions
⇨ sat in a room between two enormous fires
⇨ sat in a sewer so the bad air of the plague was driven off by the worse air of the drains
⇨ shaved a live chicken's bottom and strapped it to the plague sore[4]
⇨ … or if you didn't have a chicken handy then a poultice made of human excrement could be strapped to the sore.

---

4. Called the 'Vicary Method' after Thomas Vicary (1490–1561), an English barber-surgeon. He became surgeon to Henry VIII and won the right to dissect the cadavers of four executed criminals. The Royal College of Surgeons maintains an annual lecture in his honour. Not for the squeamish or the chicken-hearted.

The rich, in contrast, could afford a palliative against pain called 'theriac', known to the English as 'treacle' – but not treacle as we know it. Theriac was a fermentation of herbs and spices, with the occasional addition of the odd bit of snake flesh or ground Egyptian mummy. Collecting and fermenting the brew could take ten years, so it was exclusively for the rich.

Mediaeval quack doctors needed something they could make cheaply and sell as an exotic cure.

These con-artists offered …

⇨ sweet-smelling herbs thrown on a fire to clean the air
⇨ washing patients with vinegar and rose water
⇨ powders of crushed emeralds (allegedly. More likely, crushed glass)
⇨ arsenic powder or mercury (highly poisonous but fine so long as the quack took payment in advance)
⇨ letting blood out of the patient (when the patient's horoscope was right) using a barber-surgeon's razor or leeches.

Not all cures were so pleasant. Accounts exist of sufferers being coated in mercury and baked gently in the oven.

Abjuring meat, not leaving the house, not bathing, not sleeping during the day, and celibacy were all recommended. All were equally effective.

One wonder-cure that was available to all was to bathe in urine. (Whoever recommended that was surely taking the … mickey.) You don't fancy washing in your own pee and smelling like a public toilet? Worry not; there is a more pleasant alternative, since you ask. Drink a glass of your own urine twice a day. (Well, you did ask).

By the 1361–1364 outbreak, honest doctors learned how to help the patient recover by bursting the buboes till they spewed forth pus and blood. Pop those purple buboes and live.

The sincere doctors were ineffective but in mixing with the sick, caught the disease and died. They were respected among the peasantry – some of the most reputable were kidnapped to help the people of a particular district.

The dishonest quacks moved among the healthy rich, filled their purses and lived.

*Did you know ...*

There is an iconic image of plague doctors wearing a mask resembling a beak – stuffed with sweet herbs to preserve themselves. But that mask was invented in the late 1600s by Charles de l'Orme (1584 – 1678). There were NO beaked doctors around in the days of the mediaeval Black Death.

*Peasants revolting*

As a peasant you couldn't afford to run from the plague or buy crushed emeralds. But you *could* build up a resentment of the rich.

*Tyranny and anarchy are never far apart.*
> Jeremy Bentham (1748 – 1832), English
> philosopher and social reformer

The festering of peasant resentment was like the festering of plague buboes and it would be lanced thirty years after the arrival of the Black Death with The Peasants' Revolt.

## Wife-selling

*Who can find a virtuous woman? for her price is far above rubies.*
> King James Bible, Proverbs 31:10

The idea of putting a price on a woman's virtue (or simply on a woman) is heinous these days. It hasn't always been that way.

*Oh, who'll buy a wife, Says Hobbs, John Hobbs;*
*A sweet pretty wife, says Hobbs.*
*But, somehow, they tell us*
*The wife-dealing fellows*
*Were all of them sellers,*
*John Hobbs, John Hobbs.*
*And none of them wanted Jane Hobbs.*

*They settled their troubles,*
*Like most married couples,*
*John Hobbs, John Hobbs,*
*Oh, happy shoemaker, John Hobbs.*

In the opening chapter of Thomas Hardy's *The Mayor of Casterbridge* (1886) Michael Henchard sells his wife.

The London critics were scathing about this plot device. But the peasants of Hardy's rural home would have been unsurprised. It was a far more common peasant pastime than the fine folk of London (or we today) may imagine.

As Hardy himself explained:

*It may seem strange to sophisticated minds that a sane young matron could believe in the seriousness of such a transfer. But she was by no means the first or last peasant woman who had religiously adhered to her purchaser, as too many rural records show.*

Thomas Hardy (1840–1928), English novelist and poet,
*Mayor of Casterbridge*, Chapter 4

Divorce as we know it was not permitted until the 1857 Matrimonial Causes Act. A private bill of divorce was for the rich. Wife-selling was an alternative for the peasantry. The first recorded case was in 1553,[5] but could date to Saxon times.

To sell a wife by public auction or sale, a husband would bring his wife, often with a halter around her to resemble livestock – often to a marketplace or public house. Public auctions and sales were ritualistic and symbolic. The halter was considered a requirement to the legal process ... and in Bradford in 1558, a whip was also an essential.[6]

It sounds brutal but wasn't always. Generally, wife sales occurred with the consent of both the husband and wife. A buyer (new husband) was often already prearranged – maybe he was the wife's lover if there had been an affair.

*Sale of a Wife: A grinder named Calton sold his wife publicly in the market place, Stockport, on Monday week. She was purchased by a shop-mate of the husband for a gallon of beer. The fair one, who had a halter round her neck, seemed quite agreeable.*

*Blackburn Gazette*, 24 March 1833

The price of wives varied from a pittance to quite high sums. Goods as well as money were exchanged.

⇨ In 1832, a wife in Carlisle was sold for £1 and a Newfoundland dog.
⇨ At Selby in 1862, a wife was sold for a pint of beer.
⇨ In Ripon a wife was sold for the high amount of 25 shillings.

---

5. And one of the last ones was in Leeds in 1913, when a Leeds woman claimed to have been sold to her husband's workmate for £1.
6. No bad jokes here, please, about the wife-buyer having a quick whip-round.

⇨ In Chinner in 1696, a Maltster bought the wife of a Fuller for two-pence a pound. (Not worth her weight in gold ... but copper's the next best thing.)

⇨ A publican bought another man's wife for two gallons of gin.

Many women would have welcomed the legalisation of wife-selling – Anne Boleyn and Catherine Howard to name but two.

> *An elderly waterman named Ashton from Thorne (near Hull) went into hospital when his knees became arthritic. He returned to find his wife had taken a lover and they both agreed to her being 'sold' at an auction in Goole. The lover had to pay the best price or lose her. The bidding started at three-pence and eventually the young lover claimed her for five shillings and ninepence. Far from being gracious for her freedom the wife snapped her fingers in the old husband's face and said, 'There, you good-for-nothing. That's more than you would fetch.'*
>
> *The old man was more affable and as the happy 'bride' departed he said, 'Give us a wag of they hand, old lass, afore we part.'*
>
> The Manx Sun, 22 December 1849

(Her response was not recorded.)

The practice was illegal, but became a custom 'more honoured in the breach than the observance' (as Hamlet so eloquently put it).

For once the peasants had more liberty than their lords. When Sir Ralph de Camoys tried to sell his wife Margaret to a fellow knight, the arrangement was declared invalid by Parliament in 1302. The 1856 book by John Timbs that reported this tale said ... and you can hear the writer's outrage ...

*There has been however, in our time, a vile custom among the profligate of the lower classes, which some have magnified into law,: it is that the brute of a husband, wanting to get rid of his wife, taking her into the market on some fair day, setting her up to be bid for, and completing the bargain for half-a-crown or five shillings.*

John Timbs (1801–1875), English author, in *Things Not Generally Known, Faithfully Explained: a Book For Old and Young*, 1856

The 'thing-not-generally-known' by Mr Outraged Timbs was that the women were so often willing. The *Dorset County Chronicle* (which Thomas Hardy used for research) reported in the late 1820s that:

*At Buckland a labouring man named Charles Pearce sold his wife to a shoemaker named Elton, for £5. He delivered her in a halter in the public street. She seemed very willing. Bells rang.*

It is a perfect example of the upper classes (Timbs) having little notion of the lives of the underclasses. Ten years before Timbs wrote about the 'vile custom', Benjamin Disraeli was pointing out:

*Two nations; between whom there is no intercourse and no sympathy; who are as ignorant of each other's habits, thoughts, and feelings, as if they were dwellers in different zones, or inhabitants of different planets; who are formed by a different breeding, are fed by a different food, are ordered by different manners, and are not governed by the same laws: the rich and the poor.*

Benjamin Disraeli (1804–1881), British politician and writer, *Sybil*, 1845

Maybe Timbs hadn't read *Sybil*? But Timbs was right about it being illegal. In 1837, Joshua Jackson was imprisoned for one month with hard labour at West Riding for selling his spouse.

And if a virtuous woman's price *is* far above rubies, then what is a man worth? There are a few reported cases of a husband being sold to another woman. Jane Moffatt in Ireland (1839) confessed:

> *I purchased him from his first wife for £3 thinking him very cheap at that.*

He had had a miserable existence with his first wife, being described as 'her obedient slave'. But he wasn't exonerated of the charge of bigamy and was transported to Australia for seven years.

Holidays are notorious for romantic entanglements. In the 1880s, a married man fell in love with a young woman while on a ship to Australia. The young woman wrote to his wife in England asking if she'd sell him. The wife asked for £100 but was bartered down to £20. The happy holiday couple signed a legal agreement and married.

In Wolverhampton around that time a woman sold her husband for £5. When the money ran out she asked for him back. So he was more of a hired hand ... or hired any-other-part-of-his-body you care to name.

There have been 300 to 400 examples of wife-selling recorded. The happiness and despair each one represents cannot be measured.

> *Thank you, sir, thank you, said the bold auctioneer,*
> *Going for ten – is there nobody here*
> *Will bid any more? Is this not a bad job?*
> *Going. Going. I say – she is gone for ten bob*
> John Ashton, *Modern Street Ballads*, 1888

*Fined felonies*

Quaint crimes include some that you may not suspect. As the legal system became more complex (and parodied by Dickens in *Bleak House*) there were more ways for the underclasses in particular to offend. The following could be punished with a fine or imprisonment:

You will be fined for …

⇨ Racing your dog along the street (and betting on the winner). Three boys who trespassed onto a man's land were each fined just one penny but racing your dogs on the road would cost you a pound.
⇨ Snowballing or sliding on the pavement.
⇨ A man dressing in woman's clothes. (James Wilson got away with a fine of 2 shillings and 6 pence for dressing as a woman.)
⇨ Shaking a carpet in the street after 9 a.m. (It was OK before 9 a.m.)
⇨ Dumping your dead cat in the road. (You could be fined up to £5 for dumping a dead animal, rotten meat or human faeces in the street.)
⇨ Throwing orange peel on the pavement. (Throwing orange peel cost one young man a 12d fine in 1873 and another young man was fined £2 for dropping a rotten chip in the gutter in 1965 – and it's still a crime today.)
⇨ Being happy in public. (In 1873, Peter McKenna was fined £2 for whistling, singing and dancing in the street.)
⇨ Being drunk in charge of a horse and cart (which cost someone £1 in the 1860s, and being drunk in charge of a horse cost a Sunderland man a £10 fine in 1971).[7]

---

7. After a drink or few in his local the man was mocked when he claimed he owned a racehorse and kept it at the back of his car repair business. To prove his claim he went to his yard and brought the horse into the pub. A bull in a china shop would have caused less damage. (The man failed a breathalyser test.)

## Garrotting

*Fashion is only the attempt to realize art in living forms and social intercourse.*

Sir Francis Bacon (1561–1626),
English lawyer, statesman and philosopher

Crimes are subject to fashion. The Norman era saw a plethora of poachers, Georgian Britain saw a surfeit of highwayman whilst for the Victorians of the 1860s, a new terror hit the city streets – a glut of garrotters.

If you are a mugger from the underclasses you need to disable your rich victim in order to relieve them of their wealth. A gun may be beyond your means and a sock full of sand would look suspicious if you are stopped and searched by the busies on the beat.

But could they suspect you of a crime if you are simply carrying a cord or strip of leather? 'It's a lead for my little dog, h'officer ... what dog? Ah, it's lost. That's why I'm wandering the gas-lit streets looking for the poor little blighter ...'

In fact you have armed yourself with this device in order to choke your victim till they are unconscious. You can then relieve them of their wallet and watch at your leisure.

We'll never know who first came up with this idea in Victorian Britain, but it must have been a history student. An unlikely suspect, I know, but the evidence is incontrovertible. The crime was known as 'garrotting' and the term comes from the history books ...

*GARROTTING: A method of capital punishment of Spanish origin in which an iron collar is tightened around a condemned person's neck until death occurs by strangulation or by injury to the spinal column at the base of the brain.*

Dictionary

To be strictly accurate, in its original form, the cord was placed around the condemned Spaniard's neck and a stick was twisted to increase the tension. The 'garrotte' wasn't the cord – it was the name given to the stick. It had been a 'human' way of rendering someone unconscious as they were tied to a stake to be burned alive. The Inca lord Atahualpa suffered this sort of execution at the hands of the Spanish conquistadors … once he had handed over a fortune in precious metals.

Could you be a Victorian garrotter? First arm yourself with a cord – maybe fitted with a wooden handle at each end so you don't hurt your felonious hands. You are equipped to be a street robber … or a 'toby'.

Select a mark with lots of *dropsy in his pit* (or money in his wallet if you are a novice at this lark). With luck he'll be carrying a nice *kettle and tackle* (watch and chain).

Approach from behind and apply the cord to their throat and pull. First, they lose their voice, so they can't cry out, and then they lose the blood supply to the brain until they pass out.

The trick is not to tighten for too long or two hard, otherwise your victim will die. That would turn you're your mugging into murder, and the next garrotte you'd see would be the hangman's rope.

This crime became a fashion around 1862 and spread, to the terror of the toffs. Half of the garrotters came from a single profession. No, not historians with knowledge of Spanish tortures. But, as a London newspaper proclaimed:

*London is a battlefield of raging cabmen.*

Yes, your cheerful Cockney cabman had a good chance of being a garrotter in his spare time.

*Travis Bickle: I got some bad ideas in my head.*
From the movie *Taxi Driver*, 1976

By 1863 there were 115 garrotting cases in London – statistically that's 57½ committed by cab drivers – and other cities in Britain were starting to copy. Naturally there were 'honest' people who took the opportunity to make money out of people's fear. In the 1860s, a new type of men's clothing appeared:

### Scared of garrotters?

*Protect yourself with our wonderful new …*

**Leather collar**

*Wear this tough leather collar round your neck and feel safe*
*No garrotter can harm you while you wear this wonderful*
*invention.*
*Smart and comfortable too*
*Only two shillings each*

### Lindow Man

The Spanish may have given formal strangulation a name, but they didn't invent it. It's probably as old as humankind.

In 1984, a mechanical digger was cutting through turf in Lindow Moss, Cheshire when it came across a shrivelled body. Archaeologists and historians were excited by the discovery … they have a very sick idea of excitement, you understand.

The boffins declared the corpse was a Celt. The chemicals in his boggy grave land had preserved him like a pickled onion in vinegar. He is one of the only Celtic faces to be seen in modern times.

From forensic examination, his death seems to have been some sort of cruel and cut-throat Celtic sacrifice. We'll never be sure. But we do know he'd been bashed on the head, strangled, had his throat cut and thrown into the bog to drown (if he wasn't dead by then).

The garrotted guy did not get a Christian burial (and he was probably a pre-Christian victim of the Druid cult) but instead suffered the indignity of being stuck in a glass case in the British Museum for voyeuristic visitors to gawp at.

## Thuggees

The Victorian garrotters have been described as thugs … and that is more accurate than the pejorative epithet may sound. They were literally following in the footsteps of an Indian cult from 500 years before.

The earliest reference to 'thugs' is dated around 1356. The Thuggee was a secret cult whose members – Muslims and Hindus – worshipped Mother Kali, the goddess of destruction. They operated as gangs of highway robbers, tricking and later strangling their victims. They used a yellow silk or cloth scarf, which sounds a cosy way to die.

Yet 'thug' originally meant 'swindler' or 'deceiver'.

The Romans used the garrotte in the first century BC as a method of execution for traitors. The Victorian villains appear to be the first group to try to use the device to simply disable – not kill – their target.

## Putrid punishments

*It's a disagreeable thing to be whipped.*
William Tecumseh Sherman (1820–1891),
American Civil War general[8]

---

8. Noted for his scorched earth tactics, his advocacy of total war against the Native American tribes. He famously said, 'War is Hell', which is a bit like a teacher saying, 'Kids are Hell'.

Garrotter Thomas Beaumont, aged 47, was convicted of garrotting and robbing Abraham Dickenson of Batley near Dewsbury.

His sentence was twenty-four lashes followed by five years in prison. The lashing was not a pleasant experience.

The criminal was first strapped to a triangle of wood. The officer used a new cat-o'-nine-tails whip – a whip with nine strands and three hard knots at the end of each strand.

Beaumont took the first stroke in silence. After the second he cried out in pain and after the third he cried, 'Oh, dear me.'[9] As the blows followed quickly his cries grew louder. After twelve strokes his back began to show marks from the lashing. By the end of the lashing he was screaming for mercy.

The last state-sanctioned garrotting in Spain was that of a man executed for murdering a police officer in March 1974.

## Impersonating an Egyptian

'Impersonating an Egyptian' did not mean dressing up as Tutankhamen or telling people Cleopatra was your mummy. 'Egyptian' was the legal term for gypsy, so this was a law designed to stop a travelling person pretending to be a gypsy. Maybe the lawyers were worried a tramp would turn up on a doorstep and offer to read tealeaves or sell a handful of lucky heather.[10]

In England the laws of the 1710s outlawed:

*All Persons pretending to be Gipsies, or Wandering in the Habit or Form of Counterfeit Egyptians, or pretending to have Skill in Physiognomy, Palmestry, or the like Crafty Science, or*

---

9. Do we agree that 'Oh, dear me' is probably a euphemism employed by the newspaper reporter for something saltier that Beaumont bellowed?

10. If the heather is that 'lucky' how come the owners with a fistful are wandering the streets selling the stuff? Under the Trades Descriptions Act of 1968, shouldn't they be offering unlucky heather?

*pretending to tell Fortunes or like Phantastical Imaginations,*
*or using any Subtle Craft, or Unlawful Games or Plays.*

It was an offence punishable by transportation to the American colonies. The American war of Independence put a stop to that.

*The fact is, our prisons are full, and we have no way at present to dispose of the convicts.*
William Eden (1745–1814), Politician, March 1776

William Eden was opposed to transportation and campaigned against it. When the American colonies were closed to convicts, the government created the system of 'hulks' – decommissioned ships, moored in the river. Insanitary, uncomfortable and brutal.

*Punishment is not for revenge, but to lessen crime and reform the criminal.*
Elizabeth Fry (1780–1845), English prison reformer

But by 1785, Australia was open for business and transportation started again. So 'impersonating an Egyptian' could get you sent to America, onto a hulk or to Australia. But that was an improvement on the century before when it seemed gypsies were at some stage hanged for just being gypsies. The last person hanged as a wandering gypsy was in the 1650s.

The comedian Tommy Cooper wore an Egyptian fez as part of his act in the 1950s. Cooper lifted it from an Egyptian waiter's head moments before a Cairo show during the Second World War. Impersonating an Egyptian? He wasn't imprisoned but had an answer even if he had been:

*How do you get out of prison? Rub your hands together until they're sore. Then use the saw to cut through the bars.*
Tommy Cooper (1921–1984), Welsh-English comedian

Chapter 7

# Georgian Jokers and Victorian Villains

*Half of us are partly German. Half our language and culture,*
*generally, in Anglo-Saxon terms, is German.*[1]

Martin Freeman (b. 1971), English actor

In 1714, the Germans took over as monarchs of Britain, and they're
still on the throne. There was no Battle of Britain and the Brits
didn't fight them on the beaches. It was quite peaceful really. It was
a time of social inequality with as wide a gap as any in history.

BUT … the great needed the votes of the lower classes when it
came to elections for Parliament. They had to invite the farmers
into their great homes. Yeuch. The Earl of Cork whinged:

> *At election time I have to open my doors to every dirty fellow*
> *in the country that is worth forty shillings a year. All my*
> *best floors are spoiled by the hobnailed boots of the farmers*
> *stamping about them. Every room is a pig stye and the Chinese*
> *wallpaper in the drawing room stinks so terrible of punch and*
> *tobacco that it would strike you down to walk into it.*
>
> John Boyle (1707–1762), 5th Earl of Cork

Poor Earl of Cork.

---

1. An astonishingly concise analysis supported by research from that respected
statistician, Bilbo Baggins.

## *Peasant pain*

Punishments were still as barbaric as ever. In 1726, a human head turned up in a pond in Marylebone, London. The law officers didn't know who the dead head belonged to, so they stuck it on a pole and put it on show in St Margaret's churchyard in Westminster. John Hayes was identified, and his wife Catherine questioned. She was the daughter of poor parents and married pawnbroker John. After giving birth to twelve children their marriage became a little jaded. With a couple of accomplices she was found guilty. The men were hanged. But Catherine was a woman, so guilty of 'petty treason'. She was burned alive on 9 May 1726.

Catherine tried, unsuccessfully, to poison herself, and who can blame her? The executioner was supposed to strangle her as she stood chained to the stake. But the flames leapt up and burned his hands before he could finish her off. She tried to kick away the burning wood and more was thrown on. She died slowly and painfully.

Catherine was the last woman in England to be burned alive for petty treason. The burning of women's bodies *after* execution continued until 1790. This was no consolation to Catherine Hayes.

## Stocking frame wrecking[2]

> *Abraham Lincoln recognized that we could not survive as a free land when some men could decide that others were not fit to be free and should therefore be slaves.*
>
> Ronald Reagan (1911 – 2004), actor and
> 40th President of the US

---

2. Yes, that really was a peasant crime and the punishment was Draconian.

The agricultural revolution was driving the peasants from their 'cottage industries'. Doesn't that 'cottage' make it sound cosy? Chocolate-box images of happy yokels, knitting away in a thatched cottage while shoeless children frolic in the sunlit cottage garden?

Museums of the industrial age now have their re-enactors, in their laundered clothes and plump good health, explaining the era to the gawping groups of coach-tour trippers. They – the enactors and the visitors – return to their centrally heated, scented sanctuaries. It's as far from the reality as we are from the moon.

> *Work – work – work.*
> *My labour never flags;*
> *And what are its wages? A bed of straw,*
> *A crust of bread – and rags.*
> *That shattered roof – this naked floor –*
> *A table – a broken chair –*
> *And a wall so blank, my shadow I thank*
> *For sometimes falling there.*
>
> Thomas Hood (1799–1845), English poet,
> 'Song of the Shirt'

Cottage industry was paid piece rates – the more you produce, the longer the hours you work, the more you earn. And many didn't own their own cottages or machines; they were virtually slave labour to the 'managers' and the frame owners. Failure to keep up your payments would be punishable with imprisonment.

One young boy, Thomas Sanderson, went out to work when his family was reduced to eating acorns they had foraged. Children as young as five worked in gangs, digging turnips from frozen soil. Many were so hungry that they resorted to eating rats.

The invention of the steam engines meant that even the most efficient cottage labourer couldn't keep pace – or make a living – any longer. So, they gravitated to the towns and cities to work in the mass-producing factories. But they found other rural workers had the same idea. The competition for jobs meant that wages were low, and the only way a poor family could fend off starvation was for the children to work as well.

The conditions were revolting, and soon the peasants would be too.

### The tech problem

*A new report released by McKinsey & Company indicates that by 2030, as many as 800 million workers worldwide could be replaced at work by robots.*

CNBC business news television channel,
30 November 2017

If you are worried that new technology will make you redundant then you have a few options open to you. You could follow the old adage, 'If you can't beat 'em, join 'em.'[3] And thousands of peasants did begin to migrate from the green and muddy misery of the fields and rat-infested, damp cottages to the smoke-black, polluted, diseased, unsanitary, poisonous, exploitation of the factories.

Some of the ones who remained behind in their cottages followed the alternative adage, 'If you can't beat 'em, beat 'em up.' That least-logical solution to machines taking your job is to start a campaign of destroying that technology. Is your job in danger

---

3. Or the Egg Marketing Board advice is, if you can't beat them, try frying or poaching them.

from new technology, yes, you, reader? Then hit every computer with a hammer, trample every smartphone, and set fire to every fork-lift truck that you see.

But (a) you won't get very far before you're arrested and (b) you won't stop the advances of technology. Stagecoaches aren't going to replace the railways, no matter how many rails you tear up with your teeth. Stagecoach drivers are going to remain unemployed, idle and unwaged no matter how cute they look on Christmas cards.

Of course, the coming of steam and an industrial revolution was something new to the Georgian peasants. Sadly, they believed that wrecking the mass-production machines really could stop industrialisation with their bare hands. The factory owners didn't have bare hands, just fine leather gloves, but they had everything else on their side – money, the law, guns and the tide of history.

> *Technological progress is like an axe in the hands of a pathological criminal.*
>
> Albert Einstein (1879–1955),
> German-born theoretical physicist

The trouble is, the 'pathological criminals' were the rich. 'Pathological' because they had no empathy with their victims and 'criminals' with the wealth to buy and sell the law. The poor had no chance. But they tried.

### The machine wreckers

> *Capitalist production develops technology, only by sapping the original sources of all wealth – the soil and the labourer.*
>
> Karl Marx

The movement was known as the Luddite, after Ned Ludd, an apprentice who, myth would have it, smashed two stocking frames in 1779 because they were putting his master out of business. As with so many good historical stories this was a confection of legends and lies. Ned Ludd, apprentice, didn't exist. He was just a bogey man, a Halloween lantern, a scarecrow. He was:

*a tale told by an idiot, full of sound and fury, signifying nothing.*

William Shakespeare, *Macbeth*

Like his Sherwood Forest predecessor, Robin Hood, he was a symbol that the rebels could rally around like a pennant in their battles.[4]

If mythical Ned wasn't breaking the machines then *somebody* in Nottingham was, because, in 1788, the British government brought in The Protection of Stocking Frame Act. Wrecking a machine cost you seven or fourteen years' transportation to Australia (where wrecking a didgeridoo with a boomerang was a lesser offence).

That harsh law clearly didn't have the impact the Nottingham MPs wanted so they introduced a new Stocking Frame Act in 1812, when a new wave of Luddites were terrorising the mill owners. Now the punishment for wrecking a frame was death. It was a lord, making his maiden speech in the upper house, who raged against the cruelty of this escalation of punishment:

---

4. The mythical Ludd did inspire real fear, so much so that in one case, a militiaman reported seeing the dreaded general. 'He had a pike in his hand, like a serjeant's halberd, and a face that was a ghostly unnatural white.' What colour was the ale that militiaman had been imbibing?

*Are there not capital punishments sufficient on your statutes?*
*Is there not blood enough upon your penal code that more*
*must be poured forth?*

Lord George Byron (1788–1824),
English poet, peer and politician

Byron was a Nottinghamshire landowner and he made the point
that it was practically unenforceable as a crime:

*How will you carry this bill into effect? Can you commit a*
*whole county to their own prisons? Will you erect a gibbet*
*in every field, and hang up men like scarecrows, or will you*
*place the country under martial law; depopulate and lay*
*waste all around you and restore Sherwood Forest as an*
*asylum for outlaws?*

And he told the peers the death penalty wasn't much of a
deterrent to people who were in such misery they'd welcome the
relief of a rope and a drop:

*Are these the remedies for a starving and desperate populace?*
*Will the famished wretch who has braved your bayonets be*
*appalled by your gibbets? When death is a relief, and the only*
*relief it appears that you will afford him, will he be dragooned*
*into tranquillity?*

Very true.

He ended by painting a picture of the typical Luddite
'surrounded by those children for whom he is unable to procure
bread' being dragged to court. All their lordships needed were
twelve butchers for a jury.

140

Very poetic but ultimately poesy wasted on the House of Lords. As a Nonconformist minister put it a hundred years before Byron's tirade:

*None so deaf as those that will not hear. None so blind as those that will not see.*

Matthew Henry (1662–1714), Welsh miner

What pushed the gentry into such counter-terrorist measures? In Nottingham in 1811, the framework knitters, or stockingers, were angry. They had practised their arts for years and for a basic living. They trained young apprentices in the skills and took a pride in the quality of their work.

The new 'wide-frame' machines not only produced the goods quicker and cheaper but employed unskilled (low-waged) labour. The Nottingham stockingers also argued the machines produced inferior quality. They tried to argue they were fighting for the public's own benefit. Quality before price? The public preferred the benefit of their purses.

*I have never known much good done by those who affected to trade for the public good.*

Adam Smith (1723–1790), Scottish economist,
philosopher and author

In reality they were fighting to feed themselves and their families. The Napoleonic Wars were depressing trade and forcing down wages. The threat of the gallows and the gibbet didn't deter them – a measure of how desperate they were.

The Luddites' main tactic was to warn the owners of small factories to remove the frames. If the masters refused, the Luddites smashed the machines in night raids, using massive sledgehammers. Then they retired to the local tavern for a pint of ale and a song of triumph …

*Chant no more your old rhymes about bold Robin Hood,*
*His feats I but little admire,*
*I will sing the Achievements of General Ludd*
*Now the Hero of Nottinghamshire.*

But it's difficult to sing with a noose choking the life out of you.

Several large mills in the Manchester area were burnt down and up to fifty people, including women, were killed in the riots, which went on from February to May 1812.

The violence escalated when Yorkshire mill owner William Cartwright was forewarned of a Luddite attack and his guards killed three and wounded eighteen others. Soldiers killed at least five more the next day.

The Luddites tried to kill Cartwright in retaliation but killed mill owner William Horsfall instead.[5] Seventeen men were hanged in York for the crime.

In total, over a hundred Luddites were executed and the movement died with them. It seemed to establish a new principle in law – a principle where naturally the peasant was the loser – that industrialists have the right to impose new technology, without negotiation, or consultation with the workers or with society at large.

---

5. His boast that he would 'ride up to his britches in Luddite blood' may be seen as a teensy bit provocative, don't you think?

## Treason

*Treason doth never prosper, what's the reason?*
*For, if it prosper, none dare call it Treason.*

John Harington (1561–1612), English writer[6]

John Harington could have had the defeat of Richard III at Bosworth in mind when he wrote that. Henry Tudor – traitor – invaded England. King Richard III's supporters fought for him ... and lost.

So, Henry Tudor became King Henry VII and suddenly Richard's loyal troops were 'traitors'. The traitorous usurper declares his enemies traitors? That's a bit rich, Henry?

No, Henry Tudor had thought of that. He set the date of the start of his reign earlier than the battle so Richard's troops were warring against the 'king'. Lose-lose.

*Treason and murder ever kept together,*
*As two yoke-devils sworn to either's purpose.*

William Shakespeare, *Henry V*

'Treason' has been a tart of a word, lent to a curious range of misdemeanours:

⇨ Killing (or planning to kill) the king, his wife, or his heir. Obviously.
⇨ Violating the king's wife, his unmarried eldest daughter, or his heir's wife.
⇨ Making war against the king.

---

6. John Harington was a favoured godson of Queen Elizabeth I. He fell out of favour when he wrote a scurrilous translation of a classic poem. He won his way back into favour by inventing the first flushing toilet in the early 1590s. The queen must have been impressed ... she certainly didn't pooh-pooh it.

⇨ Providing aid and comfort to the king's enemies.
⇨ Counterfeiting the Great Seal or Privy Seal.
⇨ Counterfeiting English currency.

Before the 1300s, it included:

⇨ Fleeing from battle.
⇨ Predicting the death of your king or lord (Peter of Wakefield was hanged for predicting John would no longer be king by next year).

By the 1800s, treason had become a crime of convenience to keep the simmering unrest of the underclasses suppressed.

### Post-war blues

> We thank with brief thanksgiving
> Whatever gods may be
> That no life lives for ever;
> That dead men rise up never;
> That even the weariest river
> Winds somewhere safe to sea.

Algernon Charles Swinburne (1837–1909),
English poet, playwright and novelist

Even the weariest revolt must find somewhere to rest. But not just yet. The Napoleonic Wars ended at Waterloo in 1815, but instead of the recession ending, and peasant life improving, it just got worse for the underclasses.

⇨ The end of the war meant demobilisation for the troops, more men chasing jobs and adding to the unemployment problem.

144

⇨ Taxes on most commodities were raised to pay for the war so the cost of living went up as incomes fell.

⇨ New Corn Laws were designed to keep grain prices high to favour domestic producers – the rich landowners, naturally – and make foreign corn expensive even when supplies were short.

⇨ And, as it happened, a cold, wet winter of 1816 meant British corn WAS in short supply and the price of bread rose.

First came the Spa Fields riots in Middlesex, with the averred aim of taking over the government, the Tower of London and the Bank of England. The meeting claimed:

> *Four Millions in Distress …*
> *Four Millions Embarrassed …*
> *One Million-and-half fear Distress …*
> *Half-a-million live in splendid Luxury …*
> *Death would now be a relief to Millions*
> *Arrogance, Folly, and Crimes –*
>     *have brought affairs to this dread Crisis.*
>
> Placard at Spa Fields meeting

In March 1817, 25,000 textile workers met in Manchester and several hundred of them set off to petition the Prince Regent in London. (They clearly had no faith in parliamentary democracy.) The King's Dragoon Guards pursued them and several sabre chops later, the march was broken up. Only one man reached London with his petition.

The Seditious Meetings Act was passed in March 1817. What constituted 'sedition', you might ask? Well, like 'treason', pretty much anything the Lord Lieutenants of the counties fancied really.

Those stocking-makers in the East Midlands of England were still a festering boil of discontent. How to lance the boil?

In June 1817, Lord Sidmouth was a worried man. He was Home Secretary and disorder was in the very air he breathed. 'Sedition,' he must have groaned.

'Tranquility and harmony' was the watchword of the Prime Minister, Lord Liverpool. He urged Lord Sidmouth to use 'tranquillity and harmony' to smash the Luddites, grind the revolutionaries into the soil and hang anyone who so much as talked of sedition. You can just hear him: 'Tranquility and harmony, Sidmouth. That's the ticket, old chap.'

What they wanted was hangings *pour encourager les autres.*[7] The Spa Fields rioters hadn't given them the ruthless spectacle they needed.

The laws had been in place for months now … but the troublemakers were staying out of trouble. They were obeying the law. The Seditious Meetings banned unofficial public gatherings over fifty.[8]

'We've only hanged a few hotheads, that's all,' Lord Liverpool must have moaned.

Enter William J. Oliver.

*Oily Oliver*

*When sorrows come, they come not single spies, but in battalions.*

William Shakespeare, *Hamlet*

---

7. After a long and costly war against the French they may just have been reluctant to use that actual French phrase, but that's what they wanted. Examples.
8. Parts of this act remained law until the 1986 Public Order Act. A senior police officer still has the power to restrict numbers taking part in a public assembly. No one has yet applied the law to a session of Parliament, sadly.

When spies come, they come not in battalions but bring sorrows. Oliver was about forty years old and described as:

*A person of genteel appearance and good address, nearly six feet high, of erect figure, light hair, red and rather large whiskers, and a full face, a little pitted with the small-pox. His usual dress was a light fashionable coloured brown coat, black waistcoat, dark-blue mixture pantaloons, and Wellington boots.*

*Leeds Mercury*, June 1817

Obviously the Duke of Wellington's style of boots, not our rubber wellies.

Oliver toured the disaffected Midlands from Barnsley to Birmingham and spoke passionately of a march on London. William J. preached revolution yet made some remarkable escapes from arrest when rebel meetings were raided by troops.

He ended up in Derbyshire, where he met rebel leader Jeremiah Brandreth, an out-of-work stocking-maker. William J. Oliver brought encouraging news. From his travels he could confirm that 50,000 men were marching to London to storm the Tower. Brandreth's own group of protestors should join the march.

The 'revolution' began on 9 June. Brandreth had held a rallying meeting at a pub in Pentrich, The White Horse. He told his supporters he'd lead a march on Nottingham. Other marchers would join them en route. In Nottingham 'they would receive 100 guineas, bread, meat and ale.' William J. Oliver had promised that.

They would then lead an attack on the local militia barracks and arm themselves. Along with the 50,000 marchers from the north they would overthrow the government and 'overthrow poverty for ever'.

## The revolution gone wrong

*I could have done it yesterday if I hadn't a cold,*
*But since I've put this pint away I've never felt so bold.*
*So as soon as this pub closes, as soon as this pub closes,*
*As soon as this pub closes, the revolution starts.*

Alex Glasgow (1935 – 2001), English singer-songwriter

At 10 p.m. on 9 June, in heavy rain, the marchers left the pub and set out armed with scythes, pitchforks, sticks and a few guns. They knocked on farm doors and forced men to join them, but there was resistance. During one argument a servant, Robert Walters, was fatally shot.

They went on to Butterley Ironworks and demanded arms and cannon shot, but the Butterley men refused. The rebels stopped at three public houses along the way, and promised to pay landlords … after the government had fallen. Many men defected – well, it *was* raining – but a small band made it across the border into Nottinghamshire at around dawn, only to be faced with a detachment of the King's Hussars.

There was a brief scuffle; some marchers were arrested and more disappeared into the night. A report described them as:

*A picture of despair and wretchedness, none of them seeming*
*to be above the rank of labourers or working mechanics.*

A grand jury – of landowners, slave-owners and industrialists – decided the labourers and working mechanics would face charges of treason. Trial juries were packed with country gentry.

A show trial in October was a national sensation, especially when the ringleaders were sentenced to the traditional traitor's death.

*To be drawn on a hurdle to the place of execution and there be hanged by the neck, but not until they are dead, but that they should be taken down again, and that when they are yet alive their bowels should be taken out and burnt before their faces, and that afterwards their heads should be severed from their bodies, and their bodies be divided into four quarters, and their heads and quarters to be at the King's disposal.*

The sentence was commuted to hanging, then beheading after death.[9] Barbarous, but a message to would-be troublemakers. Fourteen other rebels were transported to Australia, and six more jailed.

*Judicial murder is the murder of an innocent, deliberately, and with all the pomp of holy Justice, perpetrated by people installed to prevent murder, or, if a murder has occurred, to see to it that it is punished appropriately.*

August Ludwig von Schlözer (1735 – 1809),
German historian[10]

There was debate in the press about the rights and wrongs of the 'example' being made of Pentrich men. The houses where guilty men had lived were pulled down, as was The White Horse meeting place.[11] Wives and children were put out of their

---

9. The board that was used to hold the bodies during the beheading is kept in Derby Museum.
10. August Ludwig von Schlözer's creation of the term 'judicial murder' was in reference to the beheading of Anna Göldi (1734–1782) – the last person to be executed in Europe for witchcraft. She had been hunted down and tortured and the trial twisted to ensure she faced the death sentence … for a crime that didn't even carry the death sentence.
11. Pentrich village still has the gap-toothed appearance of old houses interspersed with new ones, built years later, when the riot was long-forgotten everywhere else.

homes. Land taken from guilty men was redistributed to loyal tenants, some of whom had given evidence at the trial. The call for reform was silenced and it was to be almost twenty more years before reform was achieved.

The 50,000 marchers due to join Brandreth's bedraggled army? A fiction.

### *The sly spy*

And William J. Oliver who urged them on to their deaths? He wasn't around when the marchers set off through the Nottingham rain. Are we surprised? Probably not.

You've probably guessed: William 'The Spy' Oliver was a government plant. An *agent provocateur*. He had presented himself to the Home Office on 28 March 1817, offering his services as an informer. Sidmouth accepted his offer. William J. was vilified for his role in the Pentrich Riot and wisely decamped to South Africa, where he spent the rest of his life.

Liverpool and Sidmouth had what they wanted. Power stayed in the hands of the privileged.

Were Brandreth and his beheaded buddies right to riot? Or wrong?

### *Welsh woe*

*The prophet and the martyr do not see the hooting throng. Their eyes are fixed on the eternities.*
Benjamin Cardozo (1870–1938), American judge

If a government spy didn't set up an execution to suppress the peasants, then why not just hang someone – anyone?

The Welsh ironworkers wanted to protest against the dreadful conditions they had to live in. Tiny houses jam-packed together, disease and filth everywhere. Merthyr was crammed with 22,000 people. Twenty-five years before, there had only been 7,000.

Saturday, 13 August 1831 was the last day for Richard Lewis – commonly known as Dic Penderyn.

He was hanged at St Mary Street, outside Cardiff Castle, in front of a large crowd. Dic had been part of the Merthyr Riots back in May.

The ironworkers of Merthyr went on a march for a better wage and to try to get the vote. They marched into Merthyr and allegedly ransacked houses and robbed them. But the workers told a different story – they said law officers had taken away their furniture because the families were in debt. The so-called 'looters' were just taking back their own property.

The ironworkers went on to raid the courtroom, steal the court records and burn them in the streets. That was all the excuse the authorities needed to send in the troops. Twenty-four workers were shot dead. There was no legal action taken against the soldiers.

But sixteen soldiers were also wounded and suddenly the legal system sparked into action. Twenty-eight men and women were put on trial.

All but one were sentenced to transportation to Australia. But for some reason, Dic Penderyn was sentenced to hang. He was found guilty of stabbing and wounding a soldier – but even the soldier said he couldn't identify Penderyn as the man who stabbed him.

The two men who accused Penderyn weren't at the trial. They were two hairdressers. But Dic had just had an argument with them. They hated him. And you thought hairdressers were harmless …

*I always wanted to be a hairdresser.*

David Beckham (b. 1975),
English retired professional footballer

Dic Penderyn, on negligible evidence, was sentenced to hang. He had his hands tied behind his back and was led onto the scaffold by a minister. He called to the crowd, 'O Arglwydd, dyma ganwedd.' Our Welsh readers will know that means:

> O Arglwydd, dyma ganwedd.
> *(I am going to suffer unjustly.)*
>
> Dic Penderyn (1808–1831),
> Welsh protester on the scaffold

The hangman placed a white bag over Penderyn's head and tied his feet. He pulled the lever and there was a gasp from the crowd. Dic was twenty-three years old.

Forty years after the hanging, a man called Ieuan Parker confessed, on his deathbed, that he was the one who stabbed the soldier all those years ago.

Dic was a victim of judicial murder. He is remembered as a hero of the ironworkers. But in fact, Dic was a *miner*.

### Treasons and tribulations

> *Man comes and tills the field and lies beneath,*
> *And after many a summer dies the swan.*
>
> Alfred Lord Tennyson (1809–1892), 'Tithonus'

The charmingly titled An Act Concerning Swans, of 1482, asserted that all wild swans were owned by the monarch, and killing a swan was therefore an attack on the monarch's property and treason. If a hungry peasant was caught chewing on a leg of swan, then their swansong was to dangle from a rope. (If you were to kill a swan now you would be prosecuted under the Wildlife and Countryside Act 1981.)

Treason is such a handy catch-all term. In the time of Edward III (1312–1377), the courts often declared crimes as treason that others would consider simple felonies.

Under Edward III's laws, gathering firewood in the king's hunting grounds could be prosecuted as treason.

You may very well choose to call that tree-son. I couldn't possibly comment.

## Striking

An early predecessor of a general strike may have been the *secessio plebis* in ancient Rome. H.G. Wells described this event as:

> *The general strike of the plebeians; the plebeians seem to have invented the strike, which now makes its first appearance in history.*
>
> H.G. Wells (1866–1946), English writer, *Outline of History*[12]

Their first strike occurred because:

> *They saw with indignation their friends, who had often served the state bravely in the legions, thrown into chains and reduced to slavery at the demand of patrician creditors.*

The use of the English word 'strike' first appeared in 1768, when sailors, in support of demonstrations in London, 'struck' (or hauled down) the topgallant sails of merchant ships at port, thus crippling the ships. Reports of earlier times had used the words 'work stoppage' or 'industrial dispute'.

---

12. And who better to write accurate history than the man who invented 'The Time Machine'?

Whatever the name, it scares the governments as much as the marchers of Pentrich. And the government still uses the same tactics to defeat their enemies. They still use spies, informers and undercover plants.

### Car-crash relationships

In the 1950s, Britain striking had become a national joke, like the weather. The attitude of the workers was parodied in movies like *I'm All Right Jack*, in which Peter Sellers played the rabid and hypocritical shop steward, Fred Kite …

> *We do not and cannot accept the principle that incompetence justifies dismissal. That is victimisation.*
> Fred Kite, *I'm All Right Jack*, 1959

While Sellers parodied, the press pilloried. They vilified union leaders like Derek Robinson. He had led 523 walkouts at a Birmingham car plant during a thirty-month period and was labelled Red Robbo by the hostile press because of his communist principles. He wore the abuse like a badge of honour.

> *I can sleep sound at night because I never betrayed the workers I was elected to represent.*
> Derek Robinson (1927 – 2017), British Trade Unionist

Robinson said he was on the side of the peasants. But he was eventually sacked by the British Leyland carmakers. His crime? He put his name to a pamphlet that criticised the management. A ballot proposed a strike to reinstate Robinson. He lost, with 14,000 votes against and only 600 in favour. The peasants revolted *against* their champion. Wat Tyler didn't have that problem because he didn't have to confront hostile reporters …

154

only the swords of the Lord Mayor of London's men. Far less cutting.

A BBC documentary suggested MI5 planted an agent in the union to undermine Robinson. They wanted the unions onside. Why? So they could guarantee the launch of an important new car in their range – the Austin Allegro.

The plant in the union was a James Bond of the 1970s … but you can bet a gold finger he didn't drive an Austin Allegro.[13]

But striking wasn't always the subject of parody or plotting.

## The forgotten revolutions

*Teach a parrot the terms 'supply and demand' and you've got an economist.*

Thomas Carlyle (1795–1881), Scottish philosopher

In Scotland in the 1830s the weavers made linen from flax, but when the price of flax rose, the demand fell and they struggled to survive.

The price of cotton fell. It was shipped into the Clyde, the mill owners snapped it up and paid the impoverished weavers to operate the looms in the factories. They paid very badly.

In 1837, the Scottish factory workers decided a strike was the answer. Their rag-tag tartan army marched on Glasgow under their war cry:

*Scotland free, or a desart.*[14]

Striking workers' banner

---

13. This car's unique selling point was a stunning innovation – a square steering wheel. 'Allegro' means 'swift' – which it wasn't. It ran as if the driving wheels were square … and it turned rusty faster than a ginger cat.

14. Yes, the spelling is dodgy, but it could have been worse. It could have read, 'Scotland free or a dessert.' That would give a whole new slant on the line in Robbie Burns' famous poem, 'Great chieftain o' the pudding-race'.

The strike failed and the leaders were transported for seven years.

Still, they were better off than the previous leader, James 'Perley' Wilson. In 1820 he'd stirred up unrest among the workers on the Clyde.

### Riots and wrongs

What made the government panic so much that they provoked a rebellion in order to crush it? And why Scotland?

There was the writing of Robbie Burns, extolling the common man – he was the 'people's poet'. He had greeted the French Revolution with enthusiasm. He was caught singing the French revolutionary anthem *Ça ira* in a Dumfries theatre, rather than *God Save the King*. He composed an anthem to rebel William Wallace (1270–1305):

> *Scots wha hae wi' Wallace bled,*
> *Scots wham Bruce has aften led,*
> *Welcome tae your gory bed,*
> *Or tae victorie.*

It was a communist hymn long before communism was a political force and ends in praise of equality.

> *That Man to Man, the world o'er,*
> *Shall brothers be for a' that.*

Burns considered himself a poet who put the ideas of radical reformer Tom Paine into verse. And Tom Paine was unequivocal in his fight for freedom …

*Government, even in its best state, is but a necessary evil; in its worst state, an intolerable one.*

Thomas Paine (1737–1801), English writer,
*The Rights of Man*

Government 'evil'? So much for the House of Commons. Ouch.

What about the House of Lords, the good and the great with ancient titles?

*Titles are but nicknames, and every nickname is a title.*

Thomas Paine

Ooof. Tom Paine was the mentor, Robbie Burns the mouthpiece and Perlie Wilson the man of action. Burns and Paine were dead by 1820 but their spirit lived on in Wilson, and Wilson was the one the government could get their 'necessary evil' hands on.

In the first decade of the 1800s the average wage of a weaver halved. If your wage was halved you'd be pretty pissed off too. Unrest grew. In 1813, a general strike of around 40,000 weavers lasted over two months, until the government arrested the leaders, and their unions reluctantly returned to work.

By 1820, there was, in Scotland, a secret group called the Committee for Organising a Provisional Government. They were a new level of threat. They said they would not just overthrow the government, but had a plan in place for a new social structure of the people, by the people, for the people.

### Retribution

*Do not tell secrets to those whose faith and silence you have not already tested.*

Queen Elizabeth I

The more a movement grows, the harder it is to contain the secrets – to check who has been 'already tested'. In order to draw the secret dissenters into the open, the Georgian government sowed misinformation through a spy who would stir up trouble.

The spy spread the word that there was to be an uprising in Falkirk. James 'Perley' Wilson took the bait. He marched at the head of twenty-two rebels from the Lanarkshire village of Strathaven to join the uprising … and marched towards a waiting British Army ambush. The rebels avoided the army trap and turned back to Strathaven, but they were in the open and were captured the next day.

Wilson, this menace to society, was sixty years old and armed with a rusty sword. The British soldiers were armed with muskets. No contest. Wilson was arrested.

This rising was every bit as threatening as the Peasants' Revolt of 1381 and as well supported by the peasants of Scotland. The citizens of Greenock turned out in force to attack the soldiers who had been ordered to move the prisoners. The soldiers had to fight their way back out of the town as the crowd pelted them with stones. The army opened fire. They killed eight people, including an 8-year-old child, and injured ten others.

## Trial and terror

> *Terrorism, to me, is the use of terror for political purpose, and terror is indiscriminate murder of civilians to make a political point.*
>
> Al Franken (b. 1951), American politician

Overall, eighty-eight radicals were apprehended across Scotland and tried for high treason.[15] Wilson, along with nineteen others,

---

15. The government spy who betrayed them was John King, a weaver from Anderston. King left the meeting early, just before the entire committee was arrested.

was found guilty and sentenced to death. Seventeen of the rebels suffered the horrors of transportation to Australia (before cricket, surfing and lager had been invented). Wilson, John Baird and Andrew Hardie were to be publicly hanged.

Wilson was fastened to a wooden sledge and dragged to a scaffold in front of the law courts in Glasgow. The old man wore an open-fronted shirt over his white prison uniform and white gloves. The driver of the cart wore a black mask and carried an axe. No prizes for guessing his role in this public entertainment.

*Did you ever see such a crowd as this?*

James Wilson to his executioner

A vindictive judge (probably with a degree in History) decided old Wilson should suffer the ancient form of execution like William Wallace, to be hanged, drawn and quartered.

Wilson mounted the scaffold and several minutes later, his body was twisting and choking on the end of a rope. After half an hour, it was lowered and decapitated by the masked executioner.

The masked mauler, in keeping with the ancient tradition, held the bloody head and cried:

*This is the head of a traitor.*

The crowd booed and retorted:

*It is false, he has bled for his country. Shame. Murder.*

Reported in the *Glasgow Herald*

A crowd of 20,000 gathered to watch the gruesome spectacle and there was a large guard of Dragoon soldiers to prevent trouble.

Some of the soldiers fainted at the sight. It was decided to spare his corpse the disgrace of being cut into quarters. He was thrown into a pauper's grave in Glasgow but his niece later had the body dug up and returned to the churchyard in his Strathaven home.

Wilson's followers gave out handbills telling his true sad story that ended:

> *May the ghost of the murdered Wilson haunt the pillow of*
> *his cruel judge.*

That judge had called Wilson a 'miserable and sinful creature'. Many poor Scots will see him as a martyr for a free Scotland. The following week the rebels Baird and Hardie met a similar death in Stirling.

So, it all worked out well for the government. With the help of spies, the rebel leaders were identified, and a vicious example was made of three.

Strike over.

## Smuggling

> *If you wake at midnight, and hear a horse's feet,*
> *Don't go drawing back the blind, or looking in the street,*
> *Them that ask no questions isn't told a lie.*
> *Watch the wall my darling while the Gentlemen go by.*
>
> Rudyard Kipling, 'A Smuggler's Song'

Some crimes seem to attract a glamorous aura as time passes. Smuggling is one of them. Cheating the excise officers of a little tax is one of those 'victimless' crimes, isn't it?

The poem is supposed to be a mother talking to her little daughter. She's saying DON'T go squealing to the soldiers about these smugglers because they're really nice 'gentlemen'. Kipling's verse is described as 'such a lovely sweet poem'. You are Josephus Rex.[16]

Of course, they weren't 'gentlemen' … and most were not gentle men. They were thugs. In the slang of the day, the glamour of smuggling was just Banbury Stories, a bag of moonshine, fustian nonsense, slum, gammon, cow-slaver and, if you believe it you're as wise as Waltham's calf.

In 1748, William Galley, a tax collector, and David Charter set off to go to court. They were going to tell a judge all about the Hawkhurst smuggling gang from Kent.

They stopped for a drink where friends of the Hawkhurst gang met them. They:

⇨ got them drunk
⇨ tied their victims back to back
⇨ sat them on a horse
⇨ whipped them till Galley died
⇨ threw Galley down a 9-metre well
⇨ piled stones down the well to make sure he was dead.

Murder for the sake of cheap booze and fags? Gentlemen?
Would you 'watch the wall'?
Better not – the wall may be splashed with blood.

### The scale of the problem

*There are many thousands of sailors employed in this illicit traffic whilst great numbers are employed in removing smuggled goods from one part of the country to another.*

---

16. You are Josephus Rex meaning in the vernacular of the Georgians, 'You are Joe King'. Geddit? Oh, never mind.

*Smuggling is arrived to a height unprecedented in this or,*
*perhaps in any other nation in Europe.*

George Bishop, *Observations,*
*Remarks and Means to Prevent Smuggling,* 1783

Bishop guesstimated 60,000 men and 100,000 women and children were in the distribution chain. The women were useful as liquor 'mules'. They could carry bladders filled with spirits under their skirts … sometimes feigning pregnancy to carry more.

And smugglers' children were brought up to carry on the family business. In Polperro, Cornwall, the smugglers had a bookkeeper, Zephaniah Job. He charged 1 per cent of the profits for his services and made a fortune. But Zeph had a second important job. He taught in the local school. Smugglers were keen that their children learn the skills necessary to keep records and do currency conversions of francs and pounds. Smuggling brought more benefits to the communities than just cutting household booze and baccy budgets.

There were so many people involved nationally it was suggested that to cut smuggling you'd have to have half the population watching and reporting on the other half. So, even if the Preventive Services managed to detect their crimes, how could they arrest, try and punish that number?

And what sort of civil unrest would follow if you cut off 4 million gallons of cheap gin and over 10 million pounds of cut-price tea to the poorest segment of the population? If the Poll Tax was the spark that lit the Peasants' Revolt in 1381, then cutting off the peasants' tax-avoidance scheme could be just as explosive 400 years later.

Smuggling offered the poor a way out. Many smugglers were from the lowliest peasant stock, hoping to use their guile and initiative to make their fortunes. George Ranley of Kent was a law-abiding ploughman and carter when he uncovered a hidden cache of spirits, and that gave him the capital to set up in the smuggling business. As his enterprise grew he employed his son as his overseas agent and had large crews of seamen on standby to man the vessels. It seemed nothing could stop his venture but …

*There is no such uncertainty as a sure thing.*
Robert Burns (1759 – 1796), Scottish poet and
excise officer in Dumfries

The empire collapsed when George was arrested and transported to Tasmania. But many others like him were thriving and murdering their way to the top when necessary.

John Hurley was a customs officer at Branscombe in 1755. When he 'fell off a cliff' in suspicious circumstances, no one asked too many questions. Loyal law officers faced death every time they tried to do their duty. But other excise officers were open to bribery. When they caught a smuggling operation then cash or goods would change hands and the officer would have an attack of amnesia, as would the other worthies of the land who benefited from the crime.

*Five and twenty ponies, Trotting through the dark –*
*Brandy for the Parson. 'Baccy for the Clerk;*
*Laces for a lady, letters for a spy, And watch the wall, my*
*darling, while the Gentlemen go by.*
Rudyard Kipling, 'A Smuggler's Song'

*Did you know ...?*

One of the 'weapons' the excise officers could call upon was the informer. Potentially suicidal for the men and women who betrayed the smugglers' plans, of course.

At Marsden Bay, South Tyneside, a smuggler called John the Jibber betrayed his gang to the tax collectors. The Revenue men set a trap one stormy night.

But the smugglers defeated the tax men in a pistol fight, and took their revenge on John. Next morning he was found hanging over the cliff edge on a rope. His eyes had been pecked out by gulls.

John still haunts Marsden Bay ...

*Edinburgh violence*

*Enchanting Edinburgh shall make a delightful summer capital when we invade Britain.*

Joseph Goebbels (1897–1945), German Nazi
politician and Reich Minister of Propaganda

Smugglers brought booze into Edinburgh. It was cheap. The Scots liked that. The government didn't.

In 1736, the army started catching, arresting and executing smugglers. The people *didn't* like that. It led to trouble.

The mob were disaffected. Instances of smuggling had risen dramatically since the Act of Union in 1707. That had allowed weighty English taxes to be imposed on goods in Scotland. A malt tax in 1725 led to a sharp increase in the price of ale.[17] It provoked hatred of the English and their excisemen.

---

17. This was often in contradiction to the terms of the Union treaty. It was enough to make a Scot a nationalist. Suddenly smugglers were patriots, villains were heroes.

Edinburgh, March 1736, and crowds turned out to witness the hanging of Smuggler Wilson and his partner in crime.[18] The men had robbed an excise officer at Pittenweem.

So, unusually, the crowd were *not* there for the usual ghoulish gratification. They were there in a grim and sullen mood to see a local hero hang.

Andrew Wilson was taken from his cell in chains at 2 p.m.

*All was hush, Psalms sung, prayers put up for a long hour and upwards and the man hang'd with all decency & quietnes.*
More Culloden Papers, ed. D. Warrand, Inverness, 1927

Wilson had already tried to escape. His partner Robertson got away when the two men were taken to church the previous Sunday. Wilson started fighting the guards while Robertson made a run for it. The common people believed Wilson was a bit of a selfless martyr, giving his own freedom to save his friend's neck.

A large crowd had gathered at the Grassmarket and so Captain of the Guard, John Porteous, ordered an armed guard to escort the prisoner. The executioner managed to hang Wilson. But a trivial incident led to a disaster …

*After he was cut down and the guard drawing up to go off, some unlucky boys threw a stone or two at the hangman, which is very common, on which the brutal Porteous (who it seems had ordered his party to load their guns with ball) let drive first himself amongst the innocent mob and*

---

18. The third man involved had turned King's Evidence on the other two and saved his own neck – literally. Such disloyalty was loathed by the masses, who preferred to see a man die rather than betray a comrade. The man in question may have had a different take on the situation.

*commanded his men to follow his example which quickly cleansed the street but left three men, a boy and a woman dead upon the spot, besides several others wounded, some of whom are dead since.*

The retaliation seemed disproportionate to the crime. And it went on ...

*After this first fire he took it in his head to order another volley & killed a taylor in a window three storeys high, a young gentleman & a son of Mr Matheson the minister's and several more were dangerously wounded and all this from no more provocation than what I told you before, the throwing of a stone or two that hurt no body.*

The writer had a clear agenda to minimise the provocation and maximise the outrage.

*Believe this to be true, for I was an eye witness and within a yard or two of being shot as I sat with some gentlemen in a stabler's window opposite to the Gallows.*

And there was no neutral reporting of Porteous's conduct ...

*After this the crazy brute marched with his ragamuffins to the Guard, as if he had done nothing worth noticing but was not long there till the hue and cry rose from them that had lost friends & servants, demanding justice.*

There had been no attempt to save Wilson, to snatch his body or to attack the guards. But panicked Porteous had given the order for his soldiers to fire. If it wasn't panic then it was a serious misjudgement brought on by an excess of wine at dinner, consumed to calm his nerves.[19]

---

19. Let's hope that wine had been bought with all the excise duties paid?

Reports say the face of Porteous was red with rage. There seems little doubt he intended his men to inflict serious injury or death to the mud-throwers.

*I know you are here to kill me. Shoot, coward, you are only going to kill a man.*

> Che Guevara (1928–1967), Argentine
> Marxist revolutionary (last words)

### Captain captured

The people of Edinburgh were shocked. They said that Porteous should be arrested for murder. He was. That same afternoon.

Porteous was found guilty and sentenced to death. The Edinburgh folk were happy with that and looked forward to the execution of the pompous Porteous. But he had petitioned the queen for a pardon. The mob received news of her reply:

*I hereby grant a delay in the execution of Captain Porteous.*

> Her most Excellent Majesty, Queen Caroline

Porteous was NOT set free and he was still sentenced to hang. But the hanging had been postponed. Everyone was furious. They decided the law was too weak. They would take their own revenge.

On 7 September 1736, there was a hammering at the main gate of the Tolbooth, where Porteous was held. The guards knew it was a mob come to hang Captain Porteous but felt there was little point in resisting.

The gates were smashed and a gang of men in disguise rushed for the prison cells. Captain Porteous had thrown off his bulky clothes so he could climb up the chimney to safety. He was dragged back down and dressed in his nightshirt.

The mob dragged him through the streets and no one tried to stop them. They took him to the Grassmarket, where Andrew Wilson had been hanged. They had no time to build new gallows, so they threw the rope from a draper's shop over a dyer's pole outside another shop.

The rioters hauled Porteous up, kicking and struggling. He was lowered and stripped of his nightgown before he was hauled up again. The mob had not tied his hands and, as he struggled free, they broke his arm and shoulder. Someone else tried to set his naked foot alight. He was taken down a last time and beaten with pikes and swords before being hung up again. He died a short while later.

No one was ever convicted of the captain's murder though the government offered a £200 reward. The sympathies of the people and even of the clergy throughout Scotland were so firmly on the side of the rioters. The government meekly imposed a fine of the city of just £2,000, to be paid to Porteous's widow.

And the smuggling went on. Still does.

### Tobacco smuggling gang flooded the region with illicit cigarettes

*A GANG which flooded the North-East with an estimated 12 million bootleg cigarettes has received prison sentences totalling 13-and-a-half years.*

*Only one of the five-strong group is behind bars starting his sentence, however, as the remaining quartet were not present for their four-day trial at Durham Crown Court and are believed to be in their native Lithuania.*

*The Northern Echo*, 4 May 2018

There have been no reports of riots and lynchings in support of the smugglers. The consumers of the smuggled fags probably aren't fit enough to rise up and riot.

## Piracy

*Where there is a sea there are pirates.*

Greek proverb

*As a kid I was made to walk the plank. We couldn't afford a dog.*

Gary Delaney (b. 1973), English comedian

The pirate, like the highwayman, has been glamorised in stories, stage and movies.

The Georgians suffered a plague of piracy yet novelist Walter Scott wrote *The Pirate* just a few decades after the real-life exploits of John Gow. There are mistaken identities and (of course) a 'pirate' who turns out to be not the person everyone thinks.[20] So, he's pardoned, abandons piracy for a job in the navy and redeems himself by capturing pirates.

Even the Victorians, notorious for their stuffiness, bought into the idea of the pirate as a romantic hero. Scott's *The Pirate* is parodied in Gilbert and Sullivan's *Pirates of Penzance*. Frederick is a pirate about to leave the band now he has reached the end of his apprenticeship. The Pirate King points out that the pirates are tame and honourable compared to the world of Victorian business:

*Oh, better far to live and die Under the brave black flag I fly,*
*    Than play a sanctimonious part, with a pirate head and a pirate heart.*
*    Away to the cheating world go you, where pirates all are well-to-do;*
*    But I'll be true to the song I sing, and live and die a Pirate King.*

W.S. Gilbert (1836–1911) & Arthur Sullivan (1842–1900), lyricists and composers, *The Pirates of Penzance*

---

20. It was a mix-up when he was a child.

And in the twenty-first century, the same message is being fed to audiences:

> *You can always trust the untrustworthy because you can always trust that they will be untrustworthy. It's the trustworthy you can't trust.*
>
> Captain Jack Sparrow, character in *Pirates of the Caribbean*

Frederick in the opera is an honourable man who regrets his involvement with the pirate band.[21] The pirates turn out to be 'all noblemen who have gone wrong'. And, if you are a nobleman, that is enough to earn you a pardon.

Of course, the opera is a comedy, but the underlying message is clear: only a lower-class person could be a true villain. And even lower-class crime is forgivable.

> *When the enterprising burglar's not a-burgling,*
> *When the cut-throat isn't occupied in crime,*
> *He loves to hear the little brook a-gurgling,*
> *And listen to the merry village chime.*

*Pirates of Penzance* was first produced in Britain in 1880, eight years before Jack the Ripper brought a whole new level of meaning to the job description 'cut-throat'. The gurgling Jack heard was not that of a little brook.

The twentieth century rolled in like a pirate ship on an ocean wave, and still the world of fiction esteemed and exculpated pirates. The movies especially portrayed the pirates as misunderstood gentlemen.

---

21. It was a mix-up when he was a child. Is there an echo around here?

*We are Outlaws in our own land and homeless outcasts in any other. We are desperate men; we go to seek a desperate fortune. We are a brotherhood of buccaneers. We practise the trade of piracy on the high seas. We, the hunted, will now hunt.*

Errol Flynn in the title role of *Captain Blood*

The piratical life was an escape from the miseries of the land-lubber world. It represented nothing less than 'freedom'.

*Up that rigging, you monkeys.[22] Aloft. There's no chains to hold you now. Break out those sails and watch them fill with the wind that's carrying us all to freedom.*

*Captain Blood*

Peter Blood has been transported to America as a slave and hence his love of freedom. (He was only doing his job as a doctor and for that he was arrested and sentenced by Judge Jeffreys. Loud boos.) He becomes a pirate but only robs baddies, as you'd expect. Redemption comes when he fights the good fight for Britain against those French bounders, captures their island fortress and is made governor. He wins the heart of Lovely Arabella. (Loud hurrahs.)

And so the myth of the pirate as a gentleman of the sea is perpetuated.

*He was all the heroes in one magnificent, sexy, animal package. I just wish we had someone around today half as good as Errol Flynn.*

Jack L. Warner (1892–1978), film studio boss

---

22. Calling those putrid pirates 'monkeys' was a huge insult to monkeys.

## The truth

*There's very little admirable about being a pirate. There's very little functional about a pirate. There's very little real about a pirate.*

Will Oldham (b. 1970), American musician

Piracy *was* an escape for many poor sailors in Britain. It was quite an equal-opportunities profession. Not only could women become pirates,[23] but lower classes could rise through the ranks to become captains and even governors (like the fictional Captain Blood).

The trouble was, the underclasses who rose above their fellow pirates didn't have very advanced management skills. (They also lacked access to modern aids like counselling, anger management training and team-building facilities.)

So the psychopaths who rose to the top remained psychopaths and dangerous to anyone who literally crossed their path. Men like William Fly (d. 1726).

Fly was a small man – not as small as a fly but not much bigger than a boy. It is non-PC to say he suffered from 'Short Man Syndrome', or 'Napoleon Complex' – the idea that shorter men are overly aggressive and overcompensate for their height.[24] A few theories have debunked this theory. So William Fly did *not* suffer from it and I should not have so much as mentioned his height as it is irrelevant.

He may have been a prizefighter before he turned to sailing, but prizefighting was as murderous a 'sport' as gladiatorial

---

23. From Queen Teuta of Illyria (231 to 227 BC) to Grace O'Malley of Ireland in the days of Elizabeth I, to Anne Bonney (1700–1782) in the Caribbean.
24. So, did Napoleon suffer from the non-existent Napoleon Complex? Obviously. Because he was Napoleon. It's a paradox isn't it? It is also complex.

combat in Roman times.[25] But sailing attracted him as a better way to get rich quick.

*I was the kid who stared out the window. I fantasized myself on the deck of pirate ships – Cussler at the bridge.*
Clive Cussler (b. 1931), American author

William Fly signed on to sail with Captain John Green to West Africa on a ship called *Elizabeth*.

Green and Fly began to clash – maybe over a matter of paying the crew or maybe over Green's brutal methods of controlling his crew. Fly seized the opportunity to lead the men in a mutiny. The men waited till Captain Green lay drunk and asleep on his bed, crying:

*Upon deck, you dog, for we shall lose no more time about you.*

In an unusual demonstration of justice they invited the captain to choose his own fate and offered:

*Do you want to jump overboard or be tossed over like a sneaking rascal?*

Difficult one to answer. For an hour the captain begged for his life, but the mutineers grew tired of his grovelling, and tossed him overboard into the sea to feed the fishes. (Obviously the non-vegan fishes.)

You may think they'd have made him 'walk the plank' but that is a piratical myth. Merchant ships weren't builders' yards with supplies of suitable planks. It was much easier to simply throw

---

25. As a boxer you have to wonder if Fly was a flyweight, don't you?

your victims into the water. The captain clung to a trailing rope so one of the mutineers picked up an axe and lopped of his hand.

Thomas Jenkins, First Mate, was dragged on deck. One of the mutineers used the same axe that had been used to lop off Captain Green's hand and struck Jenkins on the shoulder, just missing his head. Jenkins was then thrown into the sea following his captain to Davy Jones's Locker.[26] He was last seen swimming and crying piteously for help. It was not forthcoming.

The crew celebrated by drinking a vat of punch and plotting their pirate careers.

Having led the mutiny it was natural that Fly should take command of the *Elizabeth*, and if Green was a harsh master then Fly would be an apt pupil.

The crew's first task was to use their embroidery skills to sew a Jolly Roger flag. They then renamed the *Elizabeth* and called her *Fame's Revenge*. Sounds more piratical.

They sailed to the coast of North Carolina and north towards New England. On the way they captured five ships in about two months. They boarded the *John and Betty* but the reward was paltry – sail cloth and muskets. There was one priceless thing on board: an experienced and able seaman named William Atkinson, who knew the North American waters well.

Fly decided to capture Atkinson and use him as his pilot. Atkinson tried to argue his way out of the forced labour but Fly simply said:

*Your palavering won't save your bacon. Go you shan't. Discharge your duty like an honest man, or I'll send you to the devil with my compliments.*

---

26. Many of Fly's mutinous contemporaries cast their officers adrift in a small boat or left them on a deserted coast. Fly was unusually murderous.

Following another disappointing capture, Fly ordered Atkinson to take them to Martha's Vineyard, which Atkinson overshot on purpose. They found themselves at Nantucket, and Fly flew off the handle. He took a pistol to shoot Atkinson. Another pirate intervened and argued Atkinson had made an honest mistake.

It was clear Fly was unreliable and incompetent. Atkinson played on the disaffection of the crew and said he'd help his new shipmates … but had no ambition to be captain himself. If they wanted rid of Fly, though, he wouldn't stand in their way.

The opportunity came when Fly sent six of his most loyal crew in a longboat to capture a rich vessel. The honest sailors who, along with Atkinson, had been enslaved, saw their chance. They grabbed Fly and clapped him in irons. He raged:

*May all the devils of hell would come and fly away with the ship.*

The devils of hell were not interested.

Fly and his pirate associates were brought before the Court of Admiralty at Boston. They were found guilty and condemned to death. Fly was one of the first executed.

Fly was visited in prison by Cotton Mather, the famous puritan preacher.[27] Mather attempted to persuade Fly to recant, to confess and attend church so he'd be spared the fires of hell.

The pirate declined. On the day of his execution, Fly jumped willing into the cart that would carry him to the scaffold in the town square. As Dick Turpin was to do thirteen years later, he joked with the spectators along the way.

Once on the scaffold, Fly took one look at the hangman's noose awaiting him, slated the hangman for doing a terrible knot and re-tied it himself. Fly slipped it around his own neck

---

27. Famous for his prosecution of witches during the Salem witch trials.

then said his final words to the crowd. Not regret for his short but murderous career, but advice:

> *All masters of vessels might take warning of the fate of the captain that he was murder'd, and to pay sailors their wages when due. Our captain and his mate used us barbarously.*

William Fly and two of his fellow pirates were hanged on 12 July 1726. A true pirate to the last, Fly urged all underclass people to stand up for themselves:

> *We poor Men can't have Justice done us. There is nothing said to our Commanders, let them never so much abuse us, and use us like Dogs.*

Brutal captains, pathetic prizes, hacking off the hands of defenceless men, getting lost at sea and mutineers being mutinied against then ending on a gallows. Can we imagine Errol Flynn portraying *any* of those non-heroic deeds?

> *Life's pretty good, and why wouldn't it be? I'm a pirate, after all.*
>
> Johnny Depp (b. 1963), American actor

No, Mr Depp. You are an actor perpetuating a lie.

## Forgery

> *Criminals look at identity theft and say only 1 in 700 criminals gets convicted of it. And they look at check forgery and they know that for every 1,400 forgers arrested, only about 123 get convicted and about 26 go to jail. So, the rewards are great,*

*but the risks are very slim. So that's one of the reasons that*
*make it very popular.*
Frank Abagnale (b. 1948), American security consultant with
history as a former confidence trickster, cheque forger and
imposter

The risks of being caught were not always as slim as Frank
Abagnale said. And the punishments could be brutal.

The most common form of forgery in the Middle Ages seems
to have been forging a lord's seal – the equivalent to a rich man's
signature today. It was classed as an 'atrocious injury' and ranked
above murder in the legal opinion of Edward I's law books.

Then, of course, there is the forger who makes a coin from a
cheap, base metal. (Or 'clips' good coins to stamp a new coin.)

The latter was a crime against the monarch whose head
decorated the dud coin, so it was treason. The punishment was
to be hanged, drawn and quartered for men or burned at the
stake for women.

*He who wishes to be rich in a day will be hanged in a year.*
Leonardo da Vinci (1452–1519), Italian artist

The hanged bit is straightforward. Your hands[28] are tied behind
your back, and wearing maybe a modest loincloth, you are
hauled up to a beam with a rope around your neck. As it tightens
around your throat it starves you of oxygen. You begin to black
out – mercifully. BUT (and here is the cruel bit) as you black
out you are lowered and fall to the ground. You begin to regain
consciousness. You are strapped to a hurdle and the executioner

---

28. When I say 'YOUR hands' I want to help you imagine the experience as if
    it were happening to you. That will help you empathise with the criminal
    … unless you are a woman.

cuts off your penis and testicles. It's not fatal, so you are well conscious of his next 'surgery' as he opens up your abdomen.

Reaching in, he removes your intestines and throws them onto a brazier. You watch them burn just as you lose consciousness again – hopefully for the final time. Your heart may be plucked out and join your intestines on the fire. You are less bothered about the beheading-and-quartering finale.

## Seal of approval

> *I never bought a man who wasn't for sale.*
> William Andrews Clark Sr. (1839–1925),
> American politician indicted in
> a bribes-for-votes scandal[29]

In the days of Henry III, a Jew named Moses Brown tried to claim that the monastery at Dunstable owed him money he'd loaned to the prior. He confidently went to court with a sealed deed to prove it.

But the wily prior was able to show that it was a seal design that hadn't been used for years, so it was a forgery. Moses was doomed – his status as a Jew would bring down so much prejudice on his head he was sent to the Tower to await hanging. A Christian forger would have escaped with a fine.

Did Moses hang? No. His community clubbed together to offer a massive bribe to the king and Moses escaped with exile from his home ... which is better than being exiled from his penis and testicles.

---

29. Clark died at the age of eighty-six with a fortune worth $4 billion by today's values. Let that be a lesson to you that crime doesn't pay. Unless you're a politician.

*What have we ear?*

> *My pride fell with my fortunes.*
> William Shakespeare, *As You Like It*

Mediaeval forgery was punished according to your religion or ability to pay a bribe. Elizabeth I's laws were clearer.

Edward Kelley was an all-round villain. He was charged with forgery at Lancaster. His punishment was to have his head placed in a pillory and his ears nailed to the wood. His ears were then chopped off and left nailed to the pillory as a warning to others. Everyone in Tudor England would know that a man without ears was a cheat and a liar. So, Kelley wore a black cap to hide the fact.

He later fell foul of an emperor in Prague and was locked in a tower. As he attempted to escape he slipped to his death. That really is falling foul.

*Monkey business*

Some of the greatest forgers in the Middle Ages were the monasteries. After all, you have to be able to write to forge a document.

Peasants with large families used their children to labour on their land and care for their animals. But too many children were extra mouths to feed and an unsustainable drain. One answer was to send the boys to be monks from the age of seven. But …

> *A habit does not a monk make*
> François Rabelais (1494 – 1553),
> French writer, physician and monk

These boys may not have had any religious inclinations, but they'd be fed and educated in return for some tiresome prayer rituals. Even God must have been bored by them.

The boys took vows of poverty, chastity and obedience, but were no more committed to them than the average peasant. Still, they grew to be literate and that made evasion of the vow of poverty a little easier.

The monks of Crowland Abbey, Lincolnshire seemed to be past masters of forgeries. In the early 1300s, another monastery claimed their land and suddenly the Crowland monks produced a document from way back in the 900s that showed their claim was legitimate. Except it wasn't, and the Crowland forgers were lucky to get away with it.

The fake deeds had clumsy errors:

⇨ They referred to people and places using 1300s terms.
⇨ They referred to monks who had studied at Oxford yet that was many years before Oxford was invented.
⇨ It noted the construction of a triangular bridge in the (alleged) 900s document, even though triangular bridges weren't invented until the 1300s.
⇨ It mentioned the monks had regularly attained ripe old ages such as 115, 142, and even 148.

The dissolution of the monasteries by the odious Henry VIII is often seen as a regrettable persecution of the innocents. The monks at Crowland were no innocents – they simply got away with their crimes of forgery.

To avoid their doom, the Crowland monks tried to win over the commissioners of the king with a gift of costly fish. (May have been better if they had been friars, perhaps?)

It didn't work. The abbey was dissolved in 1539. There had always been something fishy about their establishment.

### Deadly dealing

The law became increasingly severe on forgery and by the 1700s it was a capital crime.

*There are three things in the world that deserve no mercy, hypocrisy, fraud, and tyranny.*

Frederick William Robertson (1816–1853),

English clergyman

In 1804, Anne Hurle went to the house where her Aunt Jane was housekeeper to old Benjamin Allin of Greenwich.

Ben was ninety and had handed the power of attorney to his trusted housekeeper, Jane. Anne took advantage of this to forge a cheque for £500 made payable to herself. (That's £16,000 today.)

But the forgery of Ben's signature – not to mention the witness signatures – was clumsy. Even Aunt Jane testified that the signature was a fake. (Thanks Auntie Jane.)

The 22-year-old Anne was hanged outside the walls of Newgate Gaol.

A lesson for us all. If you're going to forge a signature, at least do a little research and try to copy the original?

### Georgian forging

Constable Plank. A name to savour.[30] In 1817 the London constables had been given the descriptions of a man and a woman who were passing forged £1 notes. Plank spotted the couple enter a pub and buy drinks worth a few pence. They handed over a pound note and pocketed the change.

---

30. You'd be forgiven for hoping his first name was Frank. Sorry to disappoint, but it was Samuel.

The couple were later arrested. The woman was Charlotte Newman and the man George Mansfield. She said she was a prostitute and a gent had paid her the note for her services. But when her home was searched, twenty-eight forged notes were found. That's a lot of sex with blokes who paid in dud pound notes.

Charlotte was stuffed. In a rare display of loyalty (or love) she told the jury that Mansfield knew nothing of the crime:

*The other prisoner is perfectly innocent and knows nothing of the transaction.*

Mansfield lived in the house where the twenty-eight forgeries had been found, he had been with Charlotte when she spent forged notes and was outside the shoe shop where she was finally arrested (obviously keeping a lookout).

It was inconceivable that Mansfield was 'perfectly innocent'. The jury found Charlotte guilty and had to find George equally guilty, didn't they? They didn't. They decided that the case against him had not been made. He was not seen to handle the notes himself. He walked from court a free man and she was sentenced to be hanged. An appeal to the bank would have the punishment transmuted to transportation and she tried that. The reply came:

*Charlotte Newman, I received your letter, but I cannot interfere in your behalf. The Governor & Directors of the Bank have considered your case & they also decline to interfere.*[31]

J.K. Westwood, New Bank

---

31. The banks often agreed to drop the prosecution for 'passing' forged notes if the prisoner pleaded guilty to the lesser charge of 'handling' a forgery. It may have been the judge, William Garrow insisted. He was a major reformer who dragged the legal system into the modern age and he coined the phrase 'innocent until proven guilty'.

On the Sunday before her execution date she attended a religious service in the prison chapel. In the centre of the aisle was her coffin. The preacher offered little comfort, saying:

*You are to suffer a dreadful and ignominious death – disgraceful to yourself, disgraceful to those you leave behind. Think of your parents' grey hairs, brought down with sorrow to the grave.*

Reverend Horace Salusbury Cotton

He ranted on about the crime of forgery:

*In a commercial nation like this, it is as mischievous as any crime that can be committed against the commonweal; for it rudely bursts asunder the links which unite such a society in the great chain of mutual credit and confidence, and is calculated to plunge the whole into distrust and confusion.*

The jail sold tickets to the public to attend these macabre services. Newgate chapel was packed that evening, as was the street around the scaffold, two days later, where Charlotte was hanged with another woman and two men.

It was a clumsy job. Charlotte's struggles went on a long time and the crowd reacted by hissing and booing. When the bodies were finally taken down, the families were allowed to collect them, minus their clothes. They were the property of the executioner, a perk on top of his fee.

### Peeler dealers

*Borrow trouble for yourself, if that's your nature, but don't lend it to your neighbours.*

Rudyard Kipling

Forgery of coins was so profitable in the era of Victorian Britain the forgers were protected by their sympathetic friends and neighbours. The forgers brought real money into the community – the wealth they generated was spent in the local shops and pubs and created jobs. That made arrests as dangerous for the law officers as they were for the criminals.

London Police Inspector Restieux was lucky to escape with his life in November 1840. He led a group of policemen into the London slums and arrested a forger. As they left the house with the forger a crowd gathered and pelted the police with stones.

The police fled with their prisoner, but the mob charged. The mob leader had a knife. Restieux wrestled with him and disarmed the man. The police escaped with their prisoner to the safety of the police station.

With the death penalty a certainty it is no wonder the forgers fought so desperately for their freedom.

The London slums were known as 'The Holy Land' – Restieux could have ended up with a holey hand.

## Bodysnatching

*The evil that is in the world almost always comes of ignorance, and good intentions may do as much harm as malevolence if they lack understanding.*
    Albert Camus (1913 – 1960), French philosopher and author

It seemed like a good idea at the time. Doctors need to understand the workings of the human body. Even artists like Leonardo da Vinci wanted to explore the workings of his subjects. And Leonardo da Vinci sought a deeper understanding. There were no provisions for artists to obtain cadavers, so they had to resort to unauthorised means, as indeed doctors sometimes did, such as grave robbing, bodysnatching, and murder.

The governments began to see the value in allowing a quota of criminals to be dissected. The Murder Act 1752 permitted the bodies of executed murderers to be dissected for anatomical research and education. It served to add to the horrors of capital punishment – we'll not only hang you, but we'll carve your body too. And an incomplete body means an incomplete soul, which can't enter heaven. (Probably.) But courts became kinder. Fewer people were being hanged.

The private medical schools lacked legal access to cadavers. Demand exceeded supply – by the start of the 1800s there were only around fifty executed corpses to meet the need for 1,500 – a business opportunity for anyone who lacked scruples and squeamishness.

The wealthy doctors wanted corpses so they let the impoverished underclasses supply them. A thriving black market arose in cadavers and body parts, leading to the creation of the profession of bodysnatching.[32]

And why not? Interfering with a grave was a misdemeanour, not a felony, and only punishable with a fine and imprisonment, not transportation or execution.[33]

---

32. Bodysnatching, taking *dead* bodies, is not be confused with the infamous practices of Burke and Hare – the notorious Irish pals who ran a lodging house in Edinburgh. They took *living* bodies and turned them into corpses that they could sell. In 1828, sixteen people were murdered for their cadavers, to be sold to anatomists. Burke and Hare are often labelled 'bodysnatchers'. They weren't.

33. A word of warning to budding sack-'em-up men and women out there. Be sure to leave behind any trinket or jewellery buried with the corpse. If you walk away with valuables then you *are* guilty of a felony and subject to much harsher penalties. Stick to *bodies* is the rule.

### Edinburgh evils

Edinburgh was a bodysnatching hotspot. The cemeteries were plagued by the Resurrectionists, or sack-'em-up men, as they became known.

The three leading members of a Scottish bodysnatching gang were known as *The Spoon, The Mole*, and *Merry Andrew*. Merry Andrew cheated the other two out of some bodysnatching money and they were angry. They planned their revenge.

*No life's worth more than any other, no sister worth less than any brother.*

Michael Franti (b. 1967), American musician

Merry Andrew's sister Sarah had just died and they planned to snatch her body and sell it to the doctors.

Imagine you are Merry Andrew. You guess what your partners are up to. What are you going to do about it?

He hid in the graveyard alone. When The Spoon and The Mole had dug up his sister he leaped out of hiding, dressed in a white sheet, pretending to be a ghost and scared them off. He even chased The Mole and The Spoon away from the cart they had waiting.

Poor little Sarah was saved from being sold by these sack-'em-up men. Andrew must have been Merry. How did he celebrate? He took his darling Sarah's body to the surgeon and sold her himself.

The Mole and The Spoon had done the hard digging work, while Merry Andrew 'borrowed' their cart to get his sister to the surgeon and collected the money.

Merry Andrew enjoyed telling the story and always had a good laugh. 'The Spoon went without his porridge that night,' he'd chuckle.

186

*Coffin carers*

There were answers to the bodysnatching craze:

⇨ Relatives and friends of someone who had just died would often watch over the body until burial. Many went on to watch over the grave after burial, to stop it being robbed.

⇨ Coffin guards often armed themselves. But accidents happen in the best of families. One watcher in a night graveyard saw a pale face staring at him through the bushes. He called out a warning but the phantom face didn't move. So the panicking pistol-wielding watcher fired … and shot a pig.

⇨ The expert bodysnatchers had a professional shortcut. Instead of digging out 2 metres x 1 metre x 2 metres depth of earth and dragging up the coffin, they only uncovered the top half of the coffin. They could then smash in the lid and pull the corpse out with ropes. To scotch this technique the graves were protected by a framework of iron bars called Mortsafes.

⇨ Desperate and energetic Resurrection men would dig a tunnel to the coffin, break open the end of the coffin and drag out the body. Watching relatives wouldn't see suspicious disturbance of the ground over the grave. Iron coffins began to be used to beat this.

⇨ One more extreme way in which families tried to beat the bodysnatchers was to turn a coffin into a bomb. If anyone opened the coffin lid, then a charge of gunpowder went off. It made a mess of the corpse, of course, but it also made a corpse of the bodysnatcher.

⇨ Aberdeen came up with 'Mort', where bodies could be left to rot (a little) until they were too decomposed for dissection.

## Bodies galore

The Anatomy Act of 1832 put an end to this gruesome trade. Yet thirty years later, there is a sad reminder that someone, somewhere, was still willing to deal in the dead and make money from misery. A gravestone in Hillsborough Park, Sheffield lies over a grave just 120 cm long by 50 cm wide. The inscription reads:

> *To the affectionate remembrance of Frank Bacon.*
> *Who departed this life April 2nd 1854, aged three years.*
> *Also Louis Bacon aged four months*
> *Buried in Wardsend Cemetery April 12th 1858.*
> *And was one of the many found in 1862.*
> *Who had been so ruthlessly disinterred*

## Corpse kidnap

Bodysnatching is not quite dead – unlike the corpses snatched. Despite the 'Save the Newchurch Guinea Pigs campaign group', bodysnatching continued to occur. The campaign became notorious in October 2004 when the remains of Christopher Hall's mother-in-law Gladys Hammond were removed from her grave in St Peter's churchyard, Yoxall (near Lichfield in Staffordshire).

After a four-year investigation by Staffordshire Police three men and one woman were jailed, not for the old bodysnatching crime, but for conspiracy to blackmail. The men received twelve years each and the woman received four years. Mrs Hammond's remains were recovered by police following information given by one of the four.

The guinea pig farm for fluffy hamsters was closed.

## Riots

*Cyfiawnder a charwyr cyfiawnder ydym ni oil*[34]

Banner of protest marchers in Newchurch,<br>West Wales

Own a piece of land and there are many ways you can make a profit from it. But charging people to cross your land is one of the less popular.

The peasant farmers of West Wales had a lot of grievances in the early 1840s ... the tithes and the rents charged by the church and the Poor Law that punished the poorest were resented. But top of the list was the tolls the farmers had to pay to pass along the roads.

The theory was fine: travellers pay a toll to walk, ride or drive along a road and the toll money goes to pay for that road's maintenance. But by 1840, the toll rights were taken over by English fat cats and the profits diverted into their fat purses.

The Welsh took to avoiding the toll gates by taking side roads. The toll owners responded by building 'side bars' – toll gates on the minor roads to catch anyone trying to dodge the main road tolls. The English absentee toll owners upped the charges of the side bars, to the fury of the natives.

By the winter of 1842, the sporadic protests became organised into a movement the rioters called 'The daughters of Rebecca'. They took the name from a verse in the Bible:

*And they blessed Rebekah and said unto her, Thou art our sister, be thou the mother of thousands of millions, and let thy seed possess the gate of those which hate them.*

Genesis 24:60

---

34. You don't need me to tell you that this Welsh banner meant 'Justice, and lovers of justice are we all.'

Possessing the gates of the toll bars was the aim. A campaign of destruction was planned that could have resulted in the rioters possessing a hangman's rope around the neck. So, they dressed as women and blackened their faces with soot or wore masks.

The spark that lit the Rebecca fire was the building of one of the sneaky side bars by the Mermaid Tavern near St Clears. The locals destroyed it. By the summer of 1843, the Rebecca ranks had swelled to 200, and this formidable force destroyed the Bolgoed toll gate.

It was only a matter of time before someone died and the unfortunate first was a young toll gate keeper, Sarah Williams. She tried to defy the wreckers but was shot dead.

### Love conquers toll

> *The jealous are troublesome to others, but a torment to themselves.*
>
> William Penn (1644–1718), English philosopher

Rioters suffer human weakness the same as the rest of us. And young John Jones fell madly in love with one of the rioter's girlfriends. He decided that if he got the boyfriend arrested and transported he could make the young woman Mrs Jones. He ran to the constables and betrayed the rioters.

He named Henry Morgan, son of Morgan Morgan of Cwm Cile Farm (north of Swansea). Captain Napier, the Chief Constable, took an inspector and two constables to the Morgan farm but met with an unforeseen problem. It was a Sunday. The devout family were horrified at the idea of the son being taken away on the Sabbath.

They refused to give him up. In the struggle, Captain Napier was assailed by the ladies of the house. They threw scalding porridge at him, and he shot one of the sons, John Morgan, in the leg.

The captain and his men had to retreat. They returned with reinforcements and took the whole family in, to Swansea jail. The charge was 'causing an affray'. Two brothers and a sister were jailed for a year.

The other two brothers faced the more serious charge of rioting. That meant deportation. Yet they escaped this harsh punishment for two reasons: the Judas, John Jones, was too afraid to testify. His neighbours had given him such a tough time he fled to Australia and failed to appear in court. John Jones's brother swore to the police that he could not possibly have been at Rhyd-y-pandy on the night of the riot. The traitor betrayed by his own family.

And, at the trial, Captain Napier was shown to be an unreliable witness. He claimed to be badly injured by the Morgans, but was seen playing cricket for Swansea Cricket Club the week after the arrests. The scorecard should have read: 'Captain Napier – caught out'.

The Morgan brothers went free. A greater blow to the rioters was a criminal gang that used the Rebecca disguises to hide their felonious activities. The gang were caught and transported, but the devout Nonconformist farmers and peasants felt tainted by association with the thugs.

Yet, before they disbanded and put away their dresses, the Rebecca Rioters achieved change. The exploitation of the fat cats was stamped out and many of the grievances were addressed.

A descendant of Morgan Morgan commented wryly on the escape from transportation:

*My ancestor Morgan Morgan was arrested and nearly transported to Australia, so I might have been Bruce Morgan, the premier of New South Wales.*

Rhodri Morgan (1929 – 2017),
First Minister of Wales 2000 to 2009

## Pocket-picking

*At last, the Dodger trod upon his toes, or ran upon his boot accidentally, while Charley Bates stumbled up against him behind; and in that one moment they took from him, with the most extraordinary rapidity, snuff-box, note-case, watch-guard, chain, shirt-pin, pocket-handkerchief, even the spectacle-case. If the old gentleman felt a hand in any one of his pockets, he cried out where it was; and then the game began all over again.*

Charles Dickens, *Oliver Twist*

Think of pickpocketing and we think of Oliver Twist's induction into the arts as a trainee with Fagin's gang. In real life the attempts at pickpocketing were far clumsier and pathetically unsuccessful.

In September 1837, Mary Ann Smith appeared in court charged with 'pocketpicking'. The constable who apprehended her was Benjamin Catmull. In the police jargon in the witness box we can hear him give his evidence:

*Catmull. I am an officer of Holborn. About half-past nine o'clock, on the 23rd of August, I was on Holborn bridge, and saw the prisoner go behind the victim, take his coat flap in her hand, and take a handkerchief from it. I crossed over and took hold of her – she straggled. I called to the prosecutor to come to the station-house, which he did. I took the handkerchief up and gave it to him.*

Her defence was predictable and weak:

*Prisoner. He said there were some girls with me, but there was not, and I was not near the gentleman. I did not pick his pocket.*

But a witness gave damning evidence:

*Witness. I saw her take the handkerchief from the prosecutor's person and put it under her shawl, and before she could drop it I took her in my arms – she dropped it in the struggle with me, and I took it up.*

The victim was only able to help by identifying the handkerchief:

*John Bailey. I live in Elizabeth-terrace, Liverpool-road. I am not in business – this is my handkerchief – I knew nothing of its being taken till the officer told me.*

When it looked bleak we can hear the desperation in her voice after 1809 years:

*Prisoner. Have mercy on me; I did not take it. He found it a good way from me, and he says there were two girls with me – if there was, how could he see me?*

She was found guilty. And her punishment for stealing a handkerchief worth 6d (2.5p)? Twelve months in prison.

Fagin would have sacked her for the crime of 'getting caught'.

### Same old

The punishments aren't working. The descendants of Mary Ann Smith still patrol the streets. The *Evening Standard* newspaper reported in 2016:

*King's Cross St Pancras has emerged as the worst Tube station for pickpocketing in figures which show that passengers in London have suffered nearly 4,000 thefts in a year.*

A tourist website encourages visitors to London with cheerful information like:

*Thieves have made a living off robbing London's tourists of their valuables while they wander through the city streets.*

Pickpockets are a real danger (they say) and offer a wonderful piece of advice:

*Tips For Avoiding Pickpockets In London.*
*Don't look like a tourist.* [35]

## Assassination

If the Peasants' Revolt of 1381 was the result of the poor resenting the rich, then it hadn't lessened much by the time of Queen Victoria (1819–1901).

She came to the throne in 1837, the year the Chartist organisation was formed. They wanted to organise petitions for peaceful changes and votes for every man. A 1-million-signature petition had no effect and a Chartist rebellion in Wales simply led to the deaths of fourteen Chartists and the organisation began to die, until, in 1840, Irishman Feargus O'Connor took charge. He brought more violent and revolutionary ideas to the Chartists.

---

35. This priceless information is passed on to you at no extra charge.

194

## Oxford crazy

*Assassin (noun)*
1. *a murderer, especially one who kills a politically prominent person for fanatical or monetary reasons.*
2. *one of an order of Muslim fanatics, active in Persia and Syria from about 1090 to 1272, whose chief object was to assassinate Crusaders.*

Edward Oxford (1822–1900) was the first of eight people who tried to assassinate Queen Victoria. On 4 May 1840, he bought a pair of pistols and began practising. A month later he took his pistols to Constitution Hill, near Buckingham Palace.

The queen was in the habit of riding in an open horse-drawn carriage, with her husband Albert, at that time. It was no secret. Maybe it ought to have been. The queen was unpopular enough and trying to win over her subjects by showing what a plucky little body she was.

As Vic drew level with Oxford, he fired both pistols. Two shots, two misses. He was grabbed by onlookers and made no attempt to escape. Quite the contrary. Like a Kenneth Williams' character in a *Carry On* movie, he declared to anyone who would listen:

*It was I, it was me that did it.*[36]

Sir Robert Peel's new police force investigated, and 'revolutionary' Chartist leaflets were found in Oxford's room. His loyal mother said his father had been an abusive alcoholic and Ed had inherited that instability. Doctors agreed and testified the boy was unstable due to 'brain disease'. Another factor could have been the shape of Ed's head, they said. Oxford was probably a mental imbecile.

---

36. His shooting was bad, but his grammar was atrocious.

The jury decided Ed was not guilty because there were no bullets found. The police were panicked. Not guilty? He'd go free and next time he may remember to put bullets in the gun.

So, in order to stitch him up, the jury were sent away to change their verdict to 'not guilty by reason of insanity'.

Insane? Then he could be locked away indefinitely. Phew. Again, the law of the rich was manipulated against the poor.

Vic was furious at this let-off. She must have raged like Chico Marx playing Fiorello …

> *Otis B. Driftwood: It's all right, that's in every contract. That's what they call a sanity clause.*
> *Fiorell: You can't fool me. There ain't no Sanity Claus.*
>
> A Night at the Opera, 1935

Victoria ought to have been grateful. She and her unpopular government were in danger of being overthrown. After the assassination attempt her popularity rose like a Bonfire Night rocket. (As had James I's popularity when Guy Fawkes attempted to assassinate the unloved Scot.)

Many years later, the wretched Oxford admitted that he did it because he wanted notoriety.

> *Fame is like a shaved pig with a greased tail, and it is only after it has slipped through the hands of some thousands, that some fellow, by mere chance, holds on to it.*
>
> Davy Crockett (1786–1836), American explorer

Two years later, 1842, and trade was bad, prices high, the poor were starving and out of work. The Chartists were more popular than ever. Their new petition had 3 million signatures and was 6 *miles* long. But again, it did them no good. Anger seethed in the slums of Britain.

### Try, try again

*If at first you don't succeed, try, try again. Then quit. There's no point in being a damn fool about it.*

W.C. Fields (1880–1946), American comedian

The next attempt took place in 1842, when Vic and Al were returning home from the Chapel Royal.

On the previous day, Albert had seen a man step out and wave a pistol, which failed to go off.

Now, if someone fired at you then you may just want to avoid the spot, would you not? But Mr Queen Victoria had a terrific plan. They would ride the *same* route at the *same* time the next day. Then, if the man took a pot at them, there would be police on hand to arrest him. As a counter-terrorism tactic this does not have a lot to recommend it, but Queen Vic went along with it.

Sure enough, the man repeated the attempt and a shot passed harmlessly by. The man was secured by a policeman. As for the royal couple:

*We felt as if a load had been taken off our hearts, and we thanked the Almighty for having preserved us a second time from so great a danger.*

Prince Albert (1819–1861), British consort

John Francis, the assailant, was sentenced to death. This was commuted. Again, her popularity rose, and later the queen said:

*It is worth being shot at – to see how much one is loved.*[37]

Queen Victoria (1819–1901), British monarch

---

37. A novel theory, not subscribed to by other tyrants like Adolf Hitler.

### Third time lucky

> *Deformed, unfinished, sent before my time*
> *Into this breathing world, scarce half made up,*
> *And that so lamely and unfashionable,*
> *That dogs bark at me, as I halt by them.*
> *And therefore, since I cannot prove a lover*
> *I am determined to prove a villain*
>
> William Shakespeare, *Richard III*

On 3 July, the day after the sentence of Francis had been commuted, the queen was shot at again. This time it was a hunchback named Bean, whose pistol misfired but was found to be loaded with bits of tobacco pipe.

He evaded capture at that moment, and for the next few weeks all the poor hunchbacks in London were given a lot of abuse. They were hooted at and accused in the public streets and had to be very ready with alibis for the particular afternoon referred to. At length, Bean was caught and sentenced to prison.

### Irish in a stew

Pistol-packing William Hamilton was a 22-year-old Irish bricklayer who fired at Queen Victoria in 1849, but there was no bullet in the pistol so he escaped with seven years' transportation. He was the most pathetic of peasantly pot-shot kids. He was raised in the poor school of the Protestant Orphan Society at Cork in Ireland.

In June 1850, the queen was returning from a visit to her uncle, the Duke of Cambridge, when a tall gentlemanly man was loitering. He was Robert Pate, aged thirty. As her carriage drove out of the gateway he rushed forward and struck the queen a sharp blow on the face with a small stick. Her Majesty's bonnet was crushed by the blow. Unlike the previous attackers he was almost a gentleman; an ex-army officer dismissed for his eccentric behaviour. Again the doctor defended him:

*I have had five interviews with Mr. Pate since this occurrence. From my own observation, and from what I have heard to-day, I believe him to be of unsound mind.*

Edward Thomas Monro, Esq., M.D.,
Old Bailey trial of Robert Pate

Another case of unsound mind and transportation. It must have been difficult finding anyone with a sound mind in Vic's Brit. Well, there was one.

Seventeen-year-old Arthur O'Connor attacked the queen in 1872. She really ought to have worn a target on her t-shirt by now. The boy waved a petition for Irish independence and a bullet-free pistol in the other. John Brown, her 'servant' (nudge-nudge, wink-wink), seized the lad and was rewarded with a gold medal and a handsome pension. Arthur was found to be sane and given a year in clink with twenty lashes of the birch.

Finally, in 1882, Roderick Maclean (aged thirty) shot at the queen at Royal Windsor. He was arrested. The prisoner, like the officer with a stick, had formerly been respectable, but had recently fallen on hard times. Another Irishman. He was found not guilty, on the ground of insanity.

Their real madness was not appreciating that shooting Queen Vic would not have changed much. Portly Edward would have come to the throne earlier than he did, but the poor would stay poor.

# Epilogue

*If you belong to the underclass, you are already guilty.*
Mason Cooley (1927 – 2002), American aphorist

*It's the same the whole world over:*
*It's the poor what gets the blame.*
*It's the rich what gets the pleasure;*
*Ain't it all a bloomin' shame.*

1800s ballad

Marx (Karl, not Groucho) argued that shows of wealth give people at the bottom a sense of injustice, a sense of anger and a sense of frustration. They resent the wealth being flaunted in front of them. But no one has managed to prevent the rich flaunting that wealth.

*With the greater part of rich people, the chief enjoyment of riches consists in the parade of riches.*

Adam Smith

Marxists believe capitalism leads to crime in the underclasses.

On 13 June 1381, thousands of armed peasants, men and women, poured over London Bridge and began attacking the people and symbols of their oppression.

The priest and rebel-leader John Ball summed up the motivation. It wasn't greed. It was equality.

Epilogue

*My good friends, things cannot go on well in England, nor ever will until everything shall be in common, when there shall be neither vassal nor lord, and all distinctions levelled; when the lords shall be no more masters than ourselves. How ill they have used us.*

John Ball, quoted in *Jean Froissart Chroniques* (1369–1400)

It was an end to the flaunting.

*If we all spring from a single father and mother, Adam and Eve, how can they claim or prove that they are lords more than us, except by making us produce and grow the wealth which they spend? They are clad in velvet and camlet lined with squirrel and ermine, while we go dressed in coarse cloth. They have the wines, the spices and the good bread: we have the rye, the husks and the straw, and we drink water. They have shelter and ease in their fine manors, and we have hardship and toil, the wind and the rain in the fields. And from us must come, from our labour, the things which keep them in luxury.*

And the solution wasn't simply destruction of the wealthy and their property. It was to negotiate a better deal for the underclasses …

*Let us go to the king, who is young, and remonstrate with him on our servitude.*

But there was always the threat …

*Let us tell the king we must have it otherwise, or that we shall find a remedy for it ourselves.*

John Ball (1338–1381), radical English priest

The Peasants' Revolt ended badly, of course. John Ball was taken prisoner at Coventry then hanged, drawn and quartered at St Albans (in the presence of young King Richard II).

His head was stuck on a pike on London Bridge, and the quarters of his body were exhibited at four different towns. An 'example' was made.

Over 400 years later, the demands of the Pentrich marchers (with threats) for a better deal for the underclass were laid out in a petition to the acting monarch. The end for the leaders was pretty much the same for Brandreth as it had been for Priest Ball.

For all the setbacks and defeats, peasants go on protesting. The lords and the establishment keep suppressing them. Not much has changed then.

Peasants go on committing crimes, robbing the rich, and some sociologists claim it is an underclass protest against the flaunting of wealth by the wealthy. Not much changes there either.

Looking on the gloomy side, the inequality may never change. For, as a cleverer bloke than me once said:

*For ye have the poor always with you.*[1]

The poor always with us? Written nearly 200 years ago. Surely it must have changed? Or maybe not …

*Malnourished, grey-looking, children are turning up to school in dirty uniforms and stuffing food in their pockets because they are living in poverty. They have grey skin and poor teeth, hair and nails.*
                    Speakers at the National Education Union conference,
                                          ITV report, 2 April 2018

---

1. And as it was Jesus who said that, and his dad is bigger than my dad, I'm not going to argue with him.

Or, looking on the silver side of the cloud, it *may* change. One man – against all odds – inspired a change.

*We must accept finite disappointment, but never lose infinite hope.*

Martin Luther King, Jr. (1929 – 4 April 1968),
American Baptist minister and civil rights activist

Just because the Peasants' Revolt and the Pentrich marchers changed nothing, it doesn't mean the link between poverty and crime can't be broken.

It takes just one person with passion and hope to bring about change.

One person. It could even be you. But if you're from the peasant class you are up against history. And if you're from the upper classes you won't want to change.

*Laws are like cobwebs, which may catch small flies, but let wasps and hornets break through.*

Jonathan Swift (1667 – 1745),
Anglo-Irish satirist, poet and cleric

All good things must come to an end. And so does this book.

**END**

# Index

# Index

# Index